HIDDEN SCARS

Hidden Scars
A Memoir by Jessica C. Perez

Published by:
Gingerbread Publishing House
ISBN/SKU: 979-8-218-53682-4
EISBN: 979-8-3304-9502-3

For permissions request, contact the publisher at:
info@gingerbreadpublishing.com

First Printing, 2024
First Edition December 2024

Cover Design by: Kathy Vargas

Printed in the United States of America

10 9 8 7 6 5 4 3 2 1

Content Warning

This work contains themes and scenes that may be unsettling or uncomfortable for some readers, including (but not limited to): violence, psychological distress, sexual abuse, child molestation, mature or intense emotional experiences and the lasting impact of trauma. Some scenes may be intense or distressing for readers who may be sensitive to these subjects. Readers discretion is advised.

HIDDEN SCARS

JESSICA PEREZ

DEDICATION

To my love, Christine, thank you for always being my rock. You've stood by me through everything, and I truly don't know where I'd be without you. You've changed my life in more ways than you'll ever know, and I appreciate you with all my heart. Your love and support have meant the world to me.

To my mom and dad, for always telling me to never give up. Your strength and belief in me have guided me through the toughest times, and I will forever be grateful for your unwavering encouragement.

To those who pushed me to share my story, thank you for believing in me when I struggled to believe in myself. Your support made this possible.

To everyone I mentioned in these pages who has touched my life in positive ways, I love you, and I am forever grateful for your presence in my journey.

And to Kathy, without you, this book wouldn't be in the world today. You made it a reality when I wanted to give up.

Finally, for those whose scars tell their stories-may you find the strength to rise.

Shattered Reflections

The room falls silent, the ceiling fan humming as it stirs a faint breeze across my skin. My reflection stares back, but it's not my face I see, it's the fractures beneath, the scars carved deep by life. They say life moves in a straight line, but I've learned it twists and turns without warning. It's not a sequences of events; it's a storm, calm one moment, a tempest the next, leaving us scrambling to stand.

I didn't expect to stand here again, back at this chapter of my story. I thought I'd left it behind, but life circles back, pulling us into moments we believed we'd outgrown or forgotten. Pain re-shapes memories, distorting what once seemed clear. My journey never followed a straight line, it twisted, dragged me into places I resisted, and forced me to confront parts of myself I didn't want to.

This isn't the story of a girl who overcame hardships in a clean, heroic arc. It's a story of raw, jagged moments, times when I broke, when the weight of the world crushed me. I want to bring you to those moments, to the nights when my world fell apart, when I doubted I'd make it to the next day.

Life isn't defined by events; it's shaped by the emotions connecting them. Joy. Pain. Anguish. Resilience. It's in the nights spent staring at the ceiling, searching for meaning in the hurt, asking why it had to be you. It's in the morning when you wake, draw a breath, and realize you're still here, still fighting.

My story doesn't unfold in order; emotions don't follow a straight line. Dark moments intersect with flashes of light, and when you think you've healed, the past drag scars back into focus.

My parents built my world. In those early years, they gave me love, safety, and stability. I remember family vacations, my father's voice cheering for his favorite team as we watched baseball together. Those moments real, filled with warmth, but beneath that warmth lay something else, a silence, an absence of the words I needed most: "I love you."

For years, silence echoed inside me, shaping the way I sought love and craved connection. My parents gave me everything, with pieces always missing. After their divorce, absence grew into a void I spent years struggling to fill.

Looking back now, shows how the foundations of my life cracked in ways I couldn't grasp at the time. The love once steady and secure, now fractured, leaving me unsteady with it. My world shifted. The years followed brought loss and moments of unbearable suffering, leaving me questioning everything, my worth, my purpose, my place in the world.

In the depths of pain, something pushed me forward. A flicker of light, a faint reminder my story continued. This chapter didn't define the whole. Life moves forward, unpredictable and unfair. I moved with every impossible step.

I want you to understand my story doesn't follow neat, expected lines of triumph over adversity. It's messy, full of contradictions, love and loss, hope and despair, joy and anguish. It twists and doubles back, a reminder the past never stays as far behind as we believe.

As you walk with me through these memories, through the shards of a life broken and rebuilt, I hope you see your own reflections in the pieces. We all carry scars, and in sharing them, we find the strength to heal.

This is my story. It begins not at the start, but here, in the middle, where light meets shadow, where the past lingers, and the future waits to unfold.

1

The Stage of Survival

The lights are blinding, but I've learned to draw strength from them. I stand at the podium, my palms pressed against its smooth surface, steadying myself as I look out at the crowd. Hundreds of faces wait for me to speak, to share my story, to make them feel something. Their expectation presses against me, but it no longer suffocates. Now, I welcome it.

I clear my throat, the sound echoing through the microphone in front of me, and I begin. "Good evening, everyone. I am Jessica Perez." My voice is steady. I've stood here before—on stages, under lights, sharing the truth of my survival. Tonight, though, is different.

My heart pounds as I recall the darkest moments threatening to consume me. The pain and fear rose like shadows, lurking and waiting to pull me back down. I remember the low points standing before me, where hope felt out of reach.

I remember the numbness, the sensation of being swallowed by darkness. I sat hands trembling, clutching the remnants of anything dulling the pain. In that rundown apartment, surrounded by empty bottles and broken dreams, I lost myself. The thin walls echoed the world outside, distant and unreachable. Cold crept through the cracks, mixing with the heat of shame and despair. I sank under the weight of my choices, fighting the current each day with nothing to grab onto.

Maybe it's because I know someone out there hears my story for the first time—lost, hopeless, as I once felt. The realization grips me. Moments of vulnerability, I connect with my past self, an echo of a girl who believed she lacked a voice.

The words flow as I speak, but my mind drifts. I can't help reflecting on how far I've come. Memories pull me back to another kind of stage—the cold, dirty floors of a rundown apartment, my body trembling, my mind screaming for relief. One night stands out: a freezing winter evening when frost invaded every corner of my soul. I sat on a grimy floor, the dim light flickering above, casting shadows moving like demons. I clutched my knees to my chest, alone, while the world outside carried on without me.

Back then, there were no lights, no applause, no crowd hanging on my every word. The quiet of isolation pressed against me, broken by the sound of my own ragged breaths.

I came close to taking the final step, believing it would bring release. I can still remember the blade catching the dim light of the room, a moment where despair edged toward finality. In that bleak space, I needed to reach out—somehow, some way.

I thought I was invincible, but the truth is, I was lost. Lost in the haze of addiction, running from the crushing weight of my own brokenness.

Now, I stand tall, sharing my story not with shame, but with strength.

I glance down at my hands, no trembling, no grasping for something to dull the pain. They are steady, open, ready to help others find the strength to fight their own battles.

As I speak, the memories flash through my mind—moments of weakness, moments of surrender, and moments of resilience.

Climbing out of the darkness took time and effort. I remember the early days of recovery—waking each morning with the sense of being reborn, yet raw and exposed. Each day became a battle against cravings tearing at my sanity, demanding I give in. I tried support groups, sitting in rooms with strangers sharing their rock-bottom moments and deepest fears. Their stories didn't resonate. I told myself I didn't belong, my situation didn't compare, and I walked out, determined to handle it all alone.

For a while, I moved forward in silence, but the darkness never stopped pressing in. Night after night, I lay in bed, staring at the ceiling, pulled toward the habits I tried to leave behind. Those moments revealed how much I isolated myself. I realized keeping everything inside became a prison, and the silence around me turned my despair into something heavier with every passing day.

I talk about those nights now, the ones I didn't think I'd survive, and the days that came after, when I learned how to live again. I tell them about the people who refused to give up on me, even when I gave up on myself, and how their persistence revealed a different path. I share the turning point—moments I realized survival meant more than staying alive. It meant reclaiming my life, climbing out of the darkness one hard-fought step at a time.

One-night haunts me still, a black hole swallowing every bit of hope. I sat on cold, cracked floor, the fluorescent lights buzzing overhead like angry bees. I looked around the room, the disarray mirroring the chaos in my mind. Bottles scattered; clothes piled high remnants of a life slipping through my fingers. I fought to recognize myself, a ghost drifting through the haze of addiction.

Laughter echoed from the street outside, cutting through the silence of my room like a cruel reminder. People lived their lives free, while I remained trapped in my own despair. That night, alone, the weight of my choices bore down on me. One path pulled me deeper into the void, an easy descent into oblivion. The other called for a fight—a fight for my life, for dreams slipping further from my grasp. In crushing stillness, something shifted. A spark flared deep inside me, fragile yet fierce, urging me to choose. And at that moment, I chose life.

The room quiets, the kind of silence tells me they're listening. It is in their faces—the recognition and understanding. Some carry this pain; others understand it for the first time. They're all here, and that matters.

I end my speech with the words I've spoken countless times before: "We are not defined by the darkest moments of our lives. We are defined by how we rise from them." Tonight, those words carry a weight reaching beyond me, touching something raw and real in the air between us.

The applause begins soft, grows, echoing through the room and vibrating in my chest. I step back from the podium, letting the moment wash over me. This is why I do this. Not for the applause, but for the connection—for the hope my story might help someone else find their way out of the darkness.

As I walk off the stage, the lights dim behind me, and I think of the woman I used to be. The one who thought she would never make it this far. The one who almost didn't. She did. I did. I tell my story not because it defines me, but because it's part of the journey that brought me here—to this stage, to this moment, alive and thriving.

My heart races, but it's not the panic that once gripped me when my life spun out of control. No, this is something else. This is purpose—a steady surge of knowing every word I spoke might save someone.

As I move through the backstage area, people stop to shake my hand or offer words of gratitude. "Your story moved me," one woman says, her voice trembling. "Thank you for sharing." I smile, understanding how to be vulnerable in front of strangers. At the edge of the crowd, a young man lingered, his eyes glistening with unshed tears. When our gazes meet, the battle he's fighting glistened in his eyes.

"I've been where you are," I tell him, stepping closer. "It gets better. Hold on." His expression shifts, uncertainty softening into fragile hope. He nodded, my words reached him.

Moments like these—small yet profound—remind me why I share my story. It's not about me; it's about the connections we build, the lives we touch, in the smallest ways.

It's in moments of connection that I understand the impact of my story. One encounter stays with me. I drove past Christopher Columbus Middle School in Clifton, NJ, the place where I grew up, filled with memories both painful and bright. Out of the corner of my eye, a young girl sitting on the curb with tears pooling in her eyes. Her expression reflected loneliness I once carried, and an overwhelming urge to stop pushed me forward. I wished back then someone reached out to me at her age.

I parked nearby, walked over to her, and introduced myself, offering to listen if she needed to talk. "My name is Mia," she said after a long pause. She shared her struggles, her sense of being invisible, and her fear things would never change. "I don't know if I can keep going," she whispered, her voice trembling under the weight of her pain. I shared parts of my own story—the times I carried the same isolation but found strength in the smallest connections.

We talked for an hour, exchanging fears and hopes. I realized my journey is more than survival, it's about reaching others, helping them find their own strength. Before we parted, I promised her she wasn't alone. I walked away believing the right words, spoken at the right time, can make all the difference.

Building on connection with Mia, I realized I wanted to reach others, to extend a hand to anyone searching for hope. That's when I turned to social media, starting with a single post on Facebook. I shared fragments of my journey—moments of struggle intertwined with moments of hope. Speaking into the void left me uncertain. Then the messages began, friends from the past reaching out, strangers offering encouragement, and people facing similar struggles finding comfort in my story.

As the weeks passed, each message and comment reminded me of my experiences carried meaning beyond survival. Through these posts, I reconnected with friends I thought I lost forever—friends who became a vital part of my support system as we rebuilt bonds and shared the highs and lows of our lives. Writing online grew into something more than I ever expected—a way to forge connections, shine light in dark places, and remind others none of us walk this journey alone.

Each post stripped away another layer of fear and doubt, transforming my story into a beacon for others still fighting through the darkness. With every share, the weight of my past lifted, showing me how my journey offers something meaningful. Now, as the applause fades and the last few people trickle out, vulnerability remains raw and unguarded.

Once the crowd thins, I slip out the side door into the cool night air. Silence surrounds me, wrapping around my body like a calming embrace, easing the adrenaline still courses through my veins. I walk toward my car, the night's events replaying over and over in my mind. Memories creep in, the way they always do after moments like this—moments when I've stripped my soul bare in front of others.

Leaning against the hood of my car, I stare at the night sky. The quiet outside doesn't match the noise in my head. The past claws at me, dragging itself into the present, even on nights like this, when triumph should outweigh the pain.

Flashbacks surge like a tidal wave. They never leave. The memories pull me back to a time when applause became a cruel mirage, something unreachable.

I close my eyes, and the images flood in again. That cramped apartment returns with vivid clarity—the peeling wallpaper, the broken blinds leaking too much sunlight when I craved darkness. The icy tile floor presses against my body, and empty bottles surround me like evidence of my slow destruction. That space became both a sanctuary and a prison, the place where I drowned out the world with substances promising escape but delivered despair.

My own voice, shaky and raw, begging for it to stop—for the pain, the craving, the guilt to fade. The needle presses into my hand, its touch making the world blur, dulling the chaos in my mind for a fleeting moment. My body sinks onto the cold, unyielding floor, each breath dragging heavier than the last. My heart pounds against my ribs, and static floods my thoughts, tightening around me like a noose. Desperation wraps itself around my chest, fed by the gnawing sense of worthlessness tearing at my insides. I sank into a place I never imagined possible. Reality hit me like icy water: I stood alone, gripping a bottle of cheap whiskey, clutching it as if it saved me.

Early recovery tested every part of me. Confronting my past ripped open wounds, I worked so hard to bury while I struggled to build something resembling a future. I remember therapy sessions where I sat raw and exposed, sharing pieces of my story I swore no one would ever hear. Some days, the urge to give up consumed me, pulling me toward the false comfort of my old life. Each time I hovered on the edge of surrender, faces appeared in my mind—friends who reached out when I thought no one cared, strangers who shared their stories, each one reminding me why I needed to keep going.

One moment stays with me. An old friend appeared out of nowhere, tears streaming down her face as she shared her struggles. Her words struck me, stirring something inside. I realized sharing my pain didn't just help me; it gave others the strength to heal too. Truth lit a spark I once believed extinguished. I no longer stood alone in this fight. Together, we reclaimed our lives.

And then comes the worst memory of all—the moment I hit rock bottom. Alone, shivering, my body fighting to survive. The walls around me closed in, crushing me with the realization: if I didn't get help, I wouldn't make it out alive. My name would join the long list of those who lost their battle against demons. Hopelessness tore through me, sharper than any blade. Addiction didn't haunt me—I waged war against myself. My identity slipped away, vanishing like a shadow cast on the wall, leaving nothing behind. I begged the universe for a sign, for something to pull me back, for a reason to keep fighting. The rabbit hole swallowed me, with no way out.

I survived. Somehow, I clawed my way out of the abyss—broken, battered, alive. Standing on this stage, I reflect on the distance I've traveled, the life I've fought to rebuild.

I open my eyes and draw a deep breath, steadying myself in the present. Crisp night air fills my lungs, rooting me in this moment. The person crushed by addiction and shattered under the weight of the world no longer controls my story. Strength fills me now. I've fought battles no one should face, and I've emerged stronger.

Survival doesn't erase scars. They remain, etched deep within me, as I stand in the light. They remind me of where I've been, of the war I fought to stay alive.

A vibration in my pocket pulls me out of my thoughts. I take out my phone and glance at the screen. A message from my friend, Melissa, appears.

You were amazing tonight. Proud of you.

A smile spreads across my face as her words settle over me. Melissa anchored me through the early days of recovery, holding me accountable and calling me out when I needed it. She believed in me when I couldn't believe in myself. Tonight, standing on stage, I wanted to make her proud.

I typed a reply: Thanks. *Couldn't have done it without you.*

Sitting with my phone in hand, I take in how far I've come. Recovery never stopped at getting clean. It meant piecing my life back together, one moment at a time. It meant forgiving myself, releasing the shame tied to choices that destroyed so much.

Above all, it meant reclaiming my voice and my purpose from the wreckage of all pain.

I glanced back at the building where I spoke. The lights glow through the windows, and faint voices carry through the air as people leave, chatting about the night's events. Some will go home and forget my speech by morning. Others might remember. Perhaps one person will sense less alone tonight because of what I shared.

I start the car and drive away, leaving the bright lights and the crowd behind. As the quiet streets stretch ahead, my headlights carve through the darkness, lighting the road. I reflect on the lessons I've gathered along the way—the struggles I've faced. Sharing my truth brings a sense of responsibility, but it also fills me with purpose.

The night sky opens wide, dotted with stars glimmering like the hopes I hold for the future. I think about my next speech, the stories I'll tell, the lives I'll reach. I want to tell them healing doesn't follow a straight path, the road twists with ups and downs, but it's also lined with unexpected joys and connections waiting to be made. In the depths of despair, there's always a spark of light waiting to ignite.

As I pull into my driveway, I take a deep breath and let the hope of the night settle within me. Tomorrow brings a new chance to inspire, to connect, and to keep moving forward. I've walked through fire, but now I stand tall, unashamed of the scars I carry.

I step out of the car and look at the stars again before heading inside. Work is waiting, stories need telling, and lives waiting to be touched.

My thoughts shift to what comes next.

Another event waits, another chance to share my story and help someone find the strength to keep going. For now, I focus on the road in front of me.

I survived. I'm still surviving. And tomorrow, I'll wake up and keep going.

Survival is a choice. Every day, I choose to keep fighting—for myself, for those still searching for light, for the future I refuse to give up on.

2

Scars Beneath the Surface

I once believed scars stayed on the surface—simple marks left behind by a cut or scrape. Time taught me otherwise. Scars run deeper than flesh. Some carve into the soul, invisible to the eye and impossible to escape. They never vanish. In still moments, they pulse beneath the surface, whispering reminders of what I've endured.

Scars carry weight, settling deep in the bones. Each one tells a story, though some cut deeper than others. Carrying them is like hauling a backpack stuffed with stones, each tied to a memory I want to erase. Some days, I forget; other days, the weight presses against me, a constant reminder of silent battles. It shapes how I navigate the world and how I interact with others, as though people can sense the burden pressing on my back.

I move through conversations with care, guarding against cracks revealing too much of who I am. These scars don't stop at my skin; they carve through my heart, shaping the person I've become. Pity lingers in the eyes of others, and I wonder whether they recognize the weight I carry. I smile in their presence, masking the turmoil within, while memories claw at me and refuse to let go.

These scars remind me of the battles I've survived; they also form walls, barriers keeping others at a distance. I wonder if I'll ever feel free again free of the shadows these memories cast.

For as long as I can remember, I've hidden my scars. Some are physical, remnants of days I want to erase. The deeper ones cut into my mind and creep through my thoughts without warning. Like now, as I sit here, staring at my reflection in the cracked mirror. Fractures splinter across the glass like a spiderweb, each line tracing a piece of my past.

The cracks scatter light, bending it into jagged colors—a rainbow born from pain. I ran a fingertip along one of the lines, following the sharp edge of the mirror, questioning how something so shattered can still reflect me. The girl staring back reveals nothing of the hell she's endured. Her mask holds firm—calm, composed, braced to face the world. Behind her eyes, shadows linger, hidden from everyone else.

I wonder how others would react if they understood. If they knew about the abuse, the nights spent crying into a pillow, the mornings when leaving the bed meant scaling a mountain. Would they pity me? Treat me as if I'm fragile, on the verge of breaking? Or would they recognize the strength required to endure, to keep moving forward no matter the cost?

We all construct masks, don't we? The ones we present to the world conceal the cracks below the surface. I've learned to smile through the chaos unraveling inside me. This illusion keeps people at a distance, steering their questions away. I am someone reliable, steady, in control. Beneath the façade, storms rage, hidden behind the walls I've built. I question if they'd perceive me the same way if the truth came spilling out.

The mask doesn't always hold. A burst of laughter collapses into tears. An eruption of anger breaks loose before I can stop it. In those moments, the armor I cling to cracks, leaving me exposed. Fear rushes in, and I scrambled to rebuild the mask, desperate to conceal what lies beneath.

This performance builds walls between me and the world. I crave connection, to let someone in, but revealing too much risks driving them away. Instead of reaching for companionship, I withdraw. I retreated further into myself, locked behind barriers I constructed with my own hands.

A saying I've always hated: "What doesn't kill you makes you stronger." It sounds comforting, like pain shapes you into someone better, someone tougher. The truth is some pain breaks you. And that's okay. Strength isn't about pretending everything is fine. It's about facing the scars and accepting the parts of yourself shaped by the damage.

Certain moments stay with me, etched into my memory like arrows piercing through innocence. Years have passed, but the memories refuse to fade. Shadows creep in at night, dragging me back to the moment everything unraveled.

I must have been eight or ten. The memory cuts deep—the creak of the door, the shuffle of footsteps. At first, I thought it a dream. The truth struck hard—too vivid, too real. His smile carves itself into my mind, soft and cold, pretending kindness while hiding cruelty.

I fought! When he grabbed me, I lashed out—kicking, scratching, pounding my small fists against him with everything I could summon. My strength faltered, unable to overcome his rough, unrelenting hands as they slammed me down and pinned me in place. His grip locked onto me like iron, pressing into my skin, choking the breath from my lungs.

My screams tore through the room, raw and desperate, but they shattered against the walls, collapsing into silence. The air devoured my voice, leaving me trapped in isolation. The bed beneath me shifted, not solid, turning into quicksand dragging me deeper with every second. Panic clawed at my chest, my heartbeat pounding like a drum, the sound of it drowning out everything else. I fought to stay above the surface, but the weight of his presence crushed me, dragging me deeper into a moment refusing to end.

I fought, I thrashed, my legs flailing, my body twisting in every direction, trying to break free. His strength overpowered mine, pinning me down, his weight crushing the air from my lungs. His breath scraped against my skin as he muttered words I couldn't understand, words I refused to hear. His hands clamped around my wrists, the force bruising them, locking me in place. Tears scorched my cheeks, the taste of salt filling my mouth as I sobbed, as I begged for it to stop.

It didn't.

The torture dragged on, each moment stretching into eternity, every second cutting into me with sharp, unbearable pain. My heart pounded in my ears, terror twisting through my veins, freezing my body in place. Air clawed at my throat, scraping away the strength I needed to scream. My voice broke apart before it reached anyone. No one came to help me.

When he stopped, his shadow loomed over me, filling the room with the weight of his presence. He stood there for a moment, unmoving, as though savoring what he took. Then he turned and walked away, his steps heavy and deliberate. The door clicked shut behind him, leaving behind an emptiness pressing down on my chest.

Silence swallowed the room, pressing into every corner, filling the space with suffocating stillness. I curled on the floor, arms locking around my trembling body, trying to hold myself together. The floor beneath me grew cold, the scent of him still hanging in the air, suffocating me with every shallow breath. Shadows moved along the walls, creeping closer, their shapes jagged and sharp.

The sounds of the room grew louder, the creak of the floor, the hiss of my breathing, the thud of my heart pounding in my ribs. The darkness alive, twisting and closing in on me, trapping me where I lay, broken and hollow. My world didn't shatter—it vanished, leaving nothing but the weight of what been taken.

No one knew. Not for years. He moved through the family, trusted and admired, his flawless mask, his true nature invisible to everyone else. Every time I looked at him, my stomach churned, bile rising in my throat, but no one noticed. Who could I tell? The truth sank into me like a stone, heavy and suffocating, burying itself deeper until it began to rot. The decay seeped through me, turning everything I touched into ash.

Laughter became a tool, something I used to mask the void inside me. I moved through the days pretending nothing happened, while the truth dragged behind me, grinding me down with every step. It refused to stay silent. The truth clawed through every wall I built, tearing into my voice, warping every connection I tried to hold. A hand brushing against my arm made my pulse race. A glance from across the room left me bracing for impact.

Trauma wraps itself around you, tightening its grip until it consumes every breath. It stalked me, creeping into every corner of my life, waiting in the quiet moments to strike. Shadows grew long and sharp, stretching behind me, circling closer, closing in with every passing moment. It never left. It never stopped pressing down, crushing me under its weight.

I thought I could outrun it, bury it so deep it disappears. Trauma doesn't work that way. It clings to you, when you think you've escaped it. It follows you like a shadow, always around, always waiting for the moment you let your guard down.

Some memories refuse to die, creeping into the edges of my mind and stalking me in moments of stillness. They cling to the corners, pressing down with their weight, waiting for me to stumble. One memory rises above the rest, sharp and unrelenting, twisting dread deep in my stomach.

The stench of antiseptic invades my senses, clinging to a sterile room, suffocating and sharp. Fluorescent lights buzzed and flickered above, washing everything in a cold, clinical glow stripped the world of color. The ticking clock hammered in my ears, each second slamming into me, trapping me deeper in the moment. The air grew thick, crushing my chest, each breath scraping against my throat as though the room itself sought to keep me.

I shrank into a child again, small and powerless, crushed under the weight of the past. My heartbeat pounded in my ears, hammering out a frantic rhythm drowning the world around me. Time twisted and dragged, each second pressing against me, heavy and unrelenting. I hovered at the edge of myself, slipping further into a void swallowing every shred of safety.

The light sliced through the blinds, harsh beams stretching across the room, carving jagged shadows into the walls. The space became a stage, cold and glaring, exposing every crack in my defenses. My isolation stood exposed, raw and unguarded. That moment stayed lodged in my mind, circling back without warning, clawing through every attempt to move forward.

The past doesn't loosen its grip. Its echoes creep into the present, twisting the ordinary into something dangerous. The creak of a door or footsteps in the hall drag me back to that night. My chest tightens, my pulse races, and I freeze, trembling, the scared little girl all over again. The faintest sounds—the rustle of wind, the scent of a familiar cologne—yank me into memories I buried, trapping me in pain refusing to let go.

Anxiety grips my chest, wrapping itself tighter with every shallow breath. Trust unravels thread by thread, pulling apart the foundation of every connection I try to make. What if they carry his cruelty too? The thought slithers into my mind without warning, twisting every interaction into treacherous ground, every moment into something fragile and uncertain.

Joy comes in fragments—a friend's laughter, sunlight warming my skin—but vanishes before I can hold on to it. The past doesn't rest. It crouches at the edges of my life, waiting to suffocate the smallest flicker of peace. Happiness fractures under the weight of memories pressing against me, jagged and relentless, carving into me with their permanence.

In crowded spaces, the noise swells, crushing my chest as the air thins around me. My practiced smile hides the chaos churning inside, a shield I've learned to wear, though it offers no real protection. I keep moving forward, carrying the scars refusing to heal. They burn beneath the surface, raw and exposed, etched into every part of who I've become. They don't remind me of what I've endured—they remind me of what I've lost.

Silence isn't an escape. It seeps into my mind, pulling helplessness, fear, and anger along with it. I want to tear it out of me, to scream until it shatters, to rip it from my chest and leave it behind forever. Instead, it clings to me, an unwelcome presence I can never escape.

I survived. The shadows remain.

Then came the moments of reprieve—the rare few who pulled me from the darkness threatening to swallow me whole. Melissa. God, Melissa became a beacon in those years. She noticed me when no one else dared, standing beside me when I lacked the strength to stand on my own. Without her, I might have disappeared, lost in a darker, colder place.

Melissa never needed to ask questions to sense my pain. She understood the fractures I tried to hide. Children have an instinct for finding the cracks in people, drawn to the vulnerabilities seeping through no matter how hard we try to conceal them. The bullies swarmed, predators circling their prey. Melissa stepped in front of them, her presence forming a barrier they refused to cross. Her loyalty radiated with a quiet force disarming their taunts before their words cut me.

Melissa became more than a friend. She offered me refuge in a world suffocating me. Our laughter echoed through the halls, breaking through the shadows following me everywhere. I think about those late-night conversations, the way she leaned forward, her eyes steady, her attention unwavering, as I shared my fears. She never flinched. She never judged. Sitting with her, I stripped away the layers of armor I built around myself, letting my truth rise to the surface for a moment.

Some days, I withdrew, hiding behind walls of false confidence. Melissa always found a way to draw me back, her kindness breaking through the fog surrounding me. She shared her own struggles, creating a space where easy to breathe, where my burdens eased, where I didn't have to carry the weight of my pain alone. In those moments, I learned the power of connection—a force steading me when everything else threatened to pull me under.

Despite her unwavering support, I avoided revealing my scars. Fear coiled inside me, a warning, exposing the truth might destroy the fragile world we shared. I hid my pain behind a practiced smile, as it gnawed at me from within. Protecting her from the weight of my darkness became my focus, shielding our friendship from the shadows of my past. As I wrestled with my emotions, the burden I carried grew heavier, as our bond deepened, layered with unspoken understanding.

One evening, years after high school, I unearthed my old beeper buried in a box of forgotten keepsakes. The sight of it pulled me back to those days with Melissa, to the years when those buzzing devices were our lifelines. In high school, before cell phones, we built a language of beeper codes, a secret system belonging to us. "07734," flipped upside down, meant "hello"—a quiet way of saying, "I'm here." Those numbers formed a bridge between us, carrying messages through the chaos of teenage life. On my hardest days, I sent "911," my wordless plea for help, or "411," asking, "What's going on?" Those digits carried meaning far beyond their shapes—they reminded me, I am not alone, when the weight of my emotions threatened to bury me.

Melissa always showed up. She found me wherever I hid, offering a hug or a knowing smile speaking volumes without a single word. Her presence eased the weight I carried. It amazes me how a handful of digits, tapped into a beeper, expressed everything my voice refused to say.

Memories of Melissa's understanding pressed against me as I held the beeper in my hand. She never needed me to explain my pain; her intuition cut through the silence. The vibration of "121" came rushing back, her way of saying, "I'm here," when words failed.

Those codes served as armor against the chaos—the bullying that stalked me at every turn. Melissa stepped between me and their taunts, her presence building a wall stopping their cruelty. Her loyalty stood firm, shielding me when I couldn't protect myself.

With someone as steadfast as Melissa, I hid my scars. I feared sharing the full weight of my pain would fracture the bond we shared. Instead, I buried everything, letting coded messages and brief smiles share the smallest fragments of what I carried. Her friendship anchored me, as it left me exposed in ways I struggled to grasp.

Clutching the beeper, pain rose from the depths, pulling confusion and fear into the present. The memories crashed over me—laughter and tears tangled together, the wounds of my past colliding with the warmth of Melissa's unwavering friendship.

Those memories remain part of me, but they did not define me.

I pulled in a sharp breath, my chest locking as memories burst through walls I thought would hold forever. Knots of pain tightened, refusing to let go. Melissa anchored me when the world crumbled. Fear pressed hard against me, the silence between us heavy, filled with everything I refused to say.

Her face surfaced in my thoughts—eyes steady, carrying a quiet understanding. I pictured her gaze tracing the cracks I tried to hide, lingering on the battles etched into my skin and the fragments of myself reclaimed from the wreckage. Strength emerged from the struggle, raw but unbroken, shaped by every piece I refused to lose.

The beeper became a bridge to the past, a tangible reminder of the bond once gave me strength. I pictured myself sending her a message again, typing "411" like we used to, waiting for her reply. The memory of her unwavering support washed over me, steady and comforting, like the warmth of a familiar embrace.

I longed to share everything with her, to strip away the mask and reveal the real me—scarred but healing, fractured but fighting to become whole again.

In that moment, I stood on the edge of reclaiming my story, ready to share the truth of my journey with Melissa. Those memories did not weigh me down as shackles. Instead, they formed the foundation for a stronger connection and the hope of a brighter future.

Yeah, right!

Refusing to lower my guard, I buried the scars deep, each fracture jagged and raw, too dangerous to expose. Sharing the truth meant stepping into a storm, every word threatening to tear apart the fragile connection holding us together. The thought of pity in her eyes—or worse, her seeing me as broken and weak—tightened my chest, each breath a struggle.

Behind the mask I built, I smiled at jokes, laughed when expected, and drifted through middle school as though nothing touched me. Each grin became armor, every laugh another wall keeping the truth hidden. The past dug its claws deeper, gripping tighter, pulling me into its darkness, whispering escape would never be mine.

As I stare at my reflection, I recognize the mask I've perfected. A version of me appearing strong, independent, and in control. Inside, though, I'm still that frightened little girl, shrinking at every shadow, bracing for the next blow. The difference now is I fight back. The past does not control me.

The scars remain, but they don't define me. They are a chapter in my story, not the whole book.

Maybe that's what life becomes in the end—a collection of scars, each one proof of battles fought and survived. They shape us, but they don't destroy us unless we let them.

I ran my fingers over the cracks in the mirror one last time, the rough edges scraping against my skin. The reflection staring back at me is still fractured, still broken. But it's also strong. Stronger than I ever thought possible. And for the first time, I'm okay with that. I'm okay with the cracks, with the imperfections. They're part of me, and I'm done hiding them.

3

Tides of Addiction

There are storms that don't bring thunder or lightning. They don't lash out with wind or howl through your bones. Instead, they creep in with a suffocating calm, a tide rising beneath the surface—unseen, unheard—until you're gasping for air. For me, the storm carried a name: addiction. The chaos began long before the first pill touched my hand, long before the first drink dulled the ache.

I learned what it meant to lose control at eight. Not over school or friends, but over what should be sacred—your body, your trust, your right to safety. My abuser wore a familiar face, one that should have meant protection. Instead, it became a mask for the monsters hiding where children are told they're safe. He didn't lurk in shadows; he lived within the light of family. Each time I crossed the threshold of his apartment in that cold, indifferent New York building, the world outside disappeared. Inside those walls, I became prey.

The betrayal cut deeper than a single set of hands. My grandmother let it unfold, her hands steady as she handed me over, a burden she wanted to discard. To her, I became his gift, bound in silence and shame. Her words still echo in my mind, cold and sharp: "Don't say anything. If you do, you'll destroy this family." She acted like my voice would ruin everything, while her silence held it all together. I swallowed the pain, stayed quiet, and let the tide rise around me.

The weight of silencing pressed tighter on my chest as years passed. I threw myself into school, friendships, and distractions, chasing anything to keep my mind from the truth. Trauma clung to me, sticking close like a shadow refusing to fade. By middle school, I wore my mask so well it became second nature. To everyone else, I was Jessica—the girl with the quick smile and loud laugh. No one noticed the fractures beneath the surface, or the nights spent staring at the ceiling, counting every agonizing second until daylight pushed the darkness away.

Melissa's gaze traced the cracks I tried so hard to hide. She found me clinging to the edge, her presence cutting through the weight pressing down on me. Her friendship became my lifeline, pulling me back from the depths. To her, I existed beyond brokenness or victim-hood. I was Jess—someone whole, someone more than the pain I carried. For the first time, I began to believe in possibility.

Her strength gave me the courage to speak. Her words from the day still echo in my mind, steady and relentless, slicing through my fear. "You need to tell them, Jess. You need to tell your parents." My chest tightened, terror coiling in my throat, choking off every thought. Melissa stayed with me, refusing to let me sink. With her beside me, I opened my mouth and released the truth. The words poured out—twisted, festering details rotting inside of me for years, filling the air between us.

My parents listened, disbelief and pain carved into their faces. For the first time, I breathed without the crushing weight on my chest. The relief didn't last. My father's family stepped in, their voices rising to silence mine. They demanded secrecy, calling for peace that wasn't mine. They did not protect me; they shielded him—the man who stole everything. Their betrayal tore into me, sharper than any blade. The people who should have defended me stood with him instead, guarding the monster who destroyed me.

Justice slipped away, disappearing like smoke, leaving me hollow. The man who tore apart my innocence walked away untouched; his crimes hidden under layers of denial. My family's betrayal cut deeper than his abuse ever managed. Their silence carved wounds inside me, leaving scars nothing would ever mend.

Anger burned in my chest, searing and unrelenting. It grew with every memory of their betrayal, burrowing deeper until it became a part of me.

I want to say those years brought healing, that the weight of my trauma lifted once my secret came out. But life doesn't work that way. Trauma doesn't dissolve when the truth is spoken. It lingers, digging in like a bruise refusing to fade. By my twenties, I escaped the pain by running straight into something darker: addiction.

At first, running carried the illusion of freedom. Bartending swept me into long nights filled with loud music and endless faces, distractions I clung to. The substances followed soon after. A few drinks, a handful of pills—enough to blur the edges of my reality. For a while, the chaos inside me settled into silence. Addiction, though, lies in whispers, promising escape while pulling you deeper into its grip. Every high came with a heavier crash, every escape wrapped me tighter in chains.

I locked the bar doors after closing, the air saturated with spilled liquor and stale smoke. The owner—a man I once trusted—blocked my way. His hands clamped onto my arms, his breath brushing against my neck as he hissed words I refused to hear. My body locked up, terror twisting through me and choking off my thoughts. The past surged forward, crashing over me, dragging me under.

I became the little girl trapped in the closet all over again...

The lock clicked as I turned the key, the sharp sound cutting through the heavy quiet of the bar. The smell of spilled liquor lingered in the air, mixing with the bitter staleness of cigarette smoke. My shoulders tensed as I moved toward the back door, eager to leave behind the suffocating weight of the night.

Footsteps creaked behind me, slow and deliberate. The hairs on the back of my neck rose, my chest tightening as I turned. "I thought everyone left," I said, forcing my voice to stay steady.

The owner stood by the bar; his figure half-hidden in the dim light. His smirk caught in the flicker of the overhead bulbs. "Wanted to check on you," he said, his voice low, smooth. He took a step closer, too close. "You've been working hard tonight. I figured you'd need someone to help you unwind."

My stomach knotted as I stepped back, trying to keep space between us. "I'm fine," I said, willing my feet to keep moving toward the door.

He shifted, cutting off my path. The air between us thickened. "Don't play hard to get," he murmured, his hand shooting out to grip my arm. His touch burned, sending a jolt through me. I froze, my muscles locking as his breath brushed against my cheek. The faint stench of alcohol clung to him. "You don't have to act tough," he whispered. "I see the way you look at me."

My heart pounded in my ears, a frantic rhythm drowning out everything else. I tried to pull away, but his grip tightened. "Let go of me," I said, my voice shaking, raw. I yanked harder, but his other hand slammed against the wall beside me, trapping me. The loud crack echoed through the empty bar, final and inescapable.

"You should be thanking me," he hissed. "A girl like you doesn't get attention for nothing."

The room spun as panic surged through me. My chest heaved, every breath a battle against the fear tightening around my ribs. Memories surged forward, vivid and relentless, dragging me back to a place I swore I'd never revisit.

The phone rang.

The shrill sound cut through the moment, jarring him. His head snapped toward the counter, the distraction enough to loosen his grip. My feet found movement again, and I stumbled back, breaking free. The phone rang again, loud and insistent, a lifeline shattering the suffocating stillness. Without looking back, I bolted for the door, the humid night swallowing me as I escaped...

Fate intervened in the form of his wife's phone call. The shrill ring cut through the air, snapping his focus long enough for me to pull free. I didn't wait for him to come back to his senses. I ran, slamming the door behind me, and didn't look back.

The night tore apart every illusion I built around myself. Not running anymore—drowning. Memories, fear, and addiction wrapped around me, pulling me under.

The weight of it all crushed me, dragging me deeper into an abyss I feared I would never escape.

The bottle weighed in my hand, its contents a silent accomplice pulling me deeper with every sip. Shadows twisted across the walls, thrown by the flickering lamp in the corner. They stretched and writhed, dragging buried ghosts into the open, the laughter of friends fading into murmurs, the warmth of love shoved away, and the jagged echoes of childhood scraping against my mind.

Whiskey burned as it slid down my throat, dragging the past into sharp focus. Nights blurred together, promises whispered in the dark dissolving by morning. *Tomorrow will be different;* I told myself again and again. Still, the cycle tightened its grip. I clung to the bottle, trying to use it as a shield against the wounds festering inside me. Each sip, though, revealed the truth: this wasn't an escape. It poisoned everything it touched, flooding my thoughts with venom and hollowing out my actions.

My gaze fell on the mirror across the room. A stranger stared back, sunken eyes surrounded by dark hollows, sleepless nights etched into every line of the reflection. The sparkle of dreams disappearing, choked by a fog smothering every trace of hope. I searched the glass for the person I once was—the one filled with ambition, the one who believed in something more. Instead, the reflection revealed an empty shell, a ghost trapped by regret, weighed down by the choices I couldn't undo.

My phone buzzed against the wooden nightstand, vibrating with urgency from a world I refused to face. The screen lit up, messages stacking one after another. Friends reaching out. Concern breaking through the cracks of the mask I wore, when I refused it myself. My fingers hovered over the screen, but the words jammed in my throat, sharp and suffocating. I set the phone aside and silenced it, choosing instead to sink deeper into the darkness.

The night dragged on, and addiction pulled tighter around me, wrapping itself into every corner of my mind. I poured another drink, the amber liquid catching the faint light, gleaming as it swirled in the glass. I raised it to my lips, hoping to drown the memories surging forward. My mother's rage came first, the belt cracking through the air, cutting through my childhood. Her words burned more than the strikes, leaving wounds deeper than any scar on my skin.

Mom's presence lingered like a shadow, impossible to escape. Her pain seeped into me, carving the path I stumbled down. I swore I would break the cycle, rise above it, and create something better. Instead, I sat there, gripping the thing pulling me under, repeating the destruction I promised to leave behind.

The memories wrapped themselves around me, thick as smoke, suffocating and relentless. They dragged me back to the child I been—small, yearning for love, desperate for warmth. Love, twisted and unreachable, never arrived the way I needed. My mother, drowning in her own torment, struck out in fear and fury, leaving behind wounds that went far deeper than skin.

I tipped the glass, the burn clawing its way down my throat, igniting heat that couldn't melt the cold tightening around my heart. Every sip brought a fleeting calm, evaporating the moment it arrived. The walls pressed closer, their shadows stretching, the silence closing in until it threatened to consume me.

The air inside our house grew sharp and tense before her anger struck, a suffocating silence stretching through every room. I would sit on the edge of my bed, my hands gripping the frayed edge of the quilt, heart hammering as I waited. My mother's footsteps echoed in the hallway, deliberate and heavy. When the snap of her belt cut through the quiet, the sound ripped through me like a blade. I braced myself, knees drawn close, knowing what was coming and powerless to stop it.

Her eyes always pinned me in place, sharp and unyielding, staring at something wrong inside me, something she wanted to erase. Every strike of the belt, her attempt to scour out the parts of me that didn't fit her idea of "normal." The parts of me she thought broken, incomplete. I didn't understand why her fury landed on me more than my siblings, why her gaze lingered on me, heavy with an accusation I struggled to name.

When the blows came, the pain went far beyond the sting on my skin. Each strike screamed a message I couldn't unhear: *You are not enough. You will never be enough.* I wondered if I disgusted her, if my struggles filled her with shame instead of compassion. Her silence about her own past left me drowning in questions. I knelt on rice for hours, the grains digging into my knees, each sharp jab a reminder of her disappointment. Not discipline—punishment, the kind meant to wear me down, to mold me into something I couldn't become.

She closed herself off, locking her emotions behind walls I never scaled. Her pain loomed over our home, heavy and suffocating, its weight shaping every part of me. I searched for answers in her anger, desperate to understand the reason behind the sharp words and bruising punishments. Nothing ever came. Her rage swallowed any trace of softness, leaving me grasping for glimpses of something human behind her cold exterior.

Her fury didn't leave marks on my skin; it carved into my sense of self, slicing through me. Each punishment an attempt to scrape something unwanted out of me, to erase what she decided didn't belong. Her silence about her own pain only deepened the confusion. On the rarest of days, regret flickered in her eyes, like a candle struggling against the wind. It never lasted. The anger always returned, burning away anything resembling remorse.

Afterward, when the shouting stopped and the house sank into a crushing stillness, I escaped into my imagination. I built entire lives in my mind where I became a person she accepted—a version of myself that didn't provoke her anger. A person who fits into the mold she wanted. Those daydreams were my refuge, but they also pulled me further from the truth. I craved her approval, but it never came. Nothing I said or did broke through the barriers she built between us.

The wounds she left ran deeper than bruises. They twisted how I understood love, reshaping trust into something fragile and dangerous. A hand reaching toward me made me flinch. A warm embrace turned rigid. I learned to fear connection, always bracing for the inevitable pain that followed. Still, I clung to her memory, held back by the fragile hope I might one day understand her. Some part of me believes if I make sense of her torment, I might forgive her.

With all her anger, I promised myself I would not carry her pain forward. I refused to let her bitterness take root in me. I would not pass on her cruelty to anyone else. Her rage stopped with me. The scars she left behind would become something else, something stronger, something that wouldn't destroy anyone.

I found my escape in the bottle. Each drink dulled the memories, numbing the ache in my chest. The burn crawled through my throat, pretending to offer peace, but it never touched the cold wrapping around me. Every sip lied to me, whispering the shame and guilt of failing to be what she wanted could disappear. The secrets I carried clung tighter with every swallow, their weight pressing down harder.

I sat in silence, the room around me still and heavy, the air thick with the ghosts of the past. Darkness coiled around me, threatening to swallow me whole. For a moment, a thought stirred—a tiny spark buried beneath the weight of it all: *Her pain doesn't have to define me. I can let it go.*

The moment passed. Reality pressed in, unrelenting and cold. I am not climbing out of this. I am sinking. The bottle in my hand didn't save me—it chained me. Every swallow pulled me further into the abyss, promising escape while tightening its grip.

The fire inside me didn't light a path forward. It consumed everything, leaving behind ash.

4

Whispers of Redemption

Fire tore through my throat, carving its way into my chest. Noise shattered, replaced by a thick, crushing silence wrapping around me. Thoughts crumbled under the weight of the heat coursing through my veins. Guilt and memories broke apart, stripped of their grip, until nothing remained but the relentless burn. Every swallow demanded another piece of me, leaving a hollow void in exchange.

The pull of the bottle tightened with each drink, dragging me further into the dark. Lies whispered control I no longer held. Time warped into an endless, shapeless mass, swallowing the difference between night and day. I fractured into fragments, scattering far from reach. Something inside demanded more, feeding the growing emptiness.

The night remains carved into memory with sharp, vivid precision. The fake ID pressed into my palm, its corners biting into sweaty skin. A bouncer blocked my path, his tattooed arms crossed over his chest. His gaze passed over me, quick and indifferent, before the door swung open. Sound crashed against me, a force rattling my bones and smothering my breath. Music pounded through the floor, shaking the walls and vibrating deep in my ribs. Lights slashed through the dark, illuminating flashes of bodies moving in unison, their energy pulsing with the beat.

The air hung heavy with the acrid scent of alcohol and sweat. Voices roared above the music, fractured and jagged, colliding with the pounding bass. Faces melted into shadows, their features lost in flickering light and shifting movement. The crowd surged, pulling me inward, enclosing me in a storm of motion. My breath caught, trapped beneath the weight of the chaos. Here, the past evaporated, and the world outside dissolved. I moved deeper, letting the crowd bury me, erasing everything else.

Each drink tightened the grip of the storm. The refuge I chased unraveled into chains, binding me to the darkness swallowing me whole. Every step forward surrendered more, leaving nothing behind.

In those wild nights, I claimed power through belonging. The older crowd pulled me into their chaos, their laughter cutting through the air, rough and unrelenting. They pressed cigarettes and pills into my hands, their faces lit with the promise of rebellion. The first rush crashed over me, sending the walls spinning and my pulse racing. Shadows gathered in the corners, their whispers scratching at my thoughts. I crushed the noise with every drag and swallow, chasing the stillness slipping through my fingers the moment it arrived.

High school turned into a string of punishing mornings and unending hangovers. My stomach twisted as I stumbled through hallways, fluorescent lights slicing into my eyes. Teachers stared with cold, unyielding gazes, their judgment heavy, their disappointment sharper than words. Each step felt heavier, the weight of their glances stripping more of me away. I let my grades crumble, my friendships fall apart, and whatever remains of myself fades into the haze. Another drink always waited, its pull louder than any consequence.

At home, my mother stormed into my room and slammed a bottle onto my dresser. "What is wrong with you? Do you care about anything? Your life? This family? Me?" Her voice cracked, trembling with rage. "You're throwing everything away. For what? For this garbage?"

She grabbed another bottle, holding it up as her hand shook. "Look at this! This is who you are now—a drunk, a liar. You don't care about school, about respect, about anything but your next drink. You're pathetic!"

Her words hit like blows, her breath ragged, tears streaming unchecked down her face. "I pray every night for you to wake up, but you don't. You never will. You're too selfish, too far gone. I'm done begging you."

She stepped closer, her face inches from mine, her voice dropping to a hiss. "You're not my daughter anymore. I don't know who you are. You want to destroy yourself? Fine. Do it. But leave me out of it. I can't watch this anymore."

She turned and walked away, her shoulders sagging under the weight of everything she carried. The room fell silent, the stillness cutting through the air like glass. Shame pressed against my chest, sharp and suffocating, but the next high silenced it before it could settle. I stayed frozen, waiting for the escape I knew would come.

I woke up in strange places more times than I could count, memories shattered and scattered beyond recognition. Every time, confusion crashed into me the moment my eyes opened. My chest heaved with uneven breaths, my pulse pounding, while questions tore through my mind. Where was I? What happened last night? Panic churned in my stomach, twisting tighter with each second, until I smothered it the way I always did. A cigarette burned between my shaking fingers, the sharp sting of alcohol scorching my throat as I drowned the fear. I shoved everything down, forcing it into the void where it vanished beneath the haze.

Smoke churned in the room, thick and choking, twisting in dark spirals clawing at my lungs. Every breath dragged in air so dense it crushed my ribs, locking my chest in a painful vise. The metallic tang of chemicals coated my tongue, sharp and bitter, spreading with every swallow until my throat been scalded. Around me, the walls rippled and buckled, their surfaces twisting as if alive. They bent inward, folding over themselves, threatening to collapse and trap me in their shifting chaos. Overhead, the ceiling dripped with dark streaks, long tendrils of shadow reaching down, curling toward me as though they meant to pull me under. My pulse hammered, relentless, each beat a pounding drum reverberating inside my skull until the pressure blurred the edges of my vision.

"You shouldn't be here," a voice whispered from nowhere. It came low and sharp, cutting through the smoke. I whipped my head toward the sound, but no one stood there. "They're watching." The voice grew louder, multiplying until it filled the room. "Run. Run. RUN."

Shapes flickered at the edges of my vision, slinking through the room with serpentine movements. They didn't hold their form—one moment they stretched into long, skeletal fingers, clawing at the air, and the next they shrank into small, skittering creatures vanishing when I tried to focus. Colors bled into one another, flowing across my vision in waves of greens and purples, pulsing with their own rhythm.

"Jess!" Another voice rang out, sharp and panicked. This one carried a familiarity hovering out of reach, slipping through my grasp. "What's wrong with you? What did you take?"

The floor beneath me surged, rolling in waves churning my stomach and threw off my balance. My body disconnected, weightless and drifting, as if the room and I moved in separate directions. My legs buckled under the pressure, muscles jerking with each pounding beat of my heart. The voices came again, their tones lower now, circling me with a suffocating presence. "You're broken," they hissed, every word sharp with mockery. "Nothing can fix this. No one will."

Panic surged, creeping through me with icy fingers burrowing beneath my skin. My arms dragged toward the ground, weighed down by pressure I couldn't escape, blurring the line between reality and hallucination. "Get off me!" I screamed, clawing at the empty air, trying to push back the invisible hands gripping my skin. Whispers brushed against my ears, soft and insidious, growing louder until the air pulsed with fractured, incoherent voices. They overlapped, breaking apart and reforming, each word splintered and warped, scraping through my thoughts and leaving raw edges behind.

The darkness arrived without warning, crashing over me in a relentless wave. It devoured the colors, the voices, the space itself, until nothing remained but a hollow void. My final thoughts shattered, slipping from my grasp as the world dissolved into silence.

When I came to, the world pressed down on me, every part of my body pinned beneath an invisible weight. The cold hit first, seeping through my skin and into my bones, as the rough concrete beneath me scraped against my bare arms and legs. The jagged surface bit into my flesh, grounding me in the moment. A deep, relentless ache throbbed in my head, sending waves of pain blurring my vision and twisted every sound into fractured echoes. I blinked, desperate to focus, but the world around me remained a smear of shifting shapes and restless shadows. They moved without form, bending and stretching into grotesque patterns beyond my comprehension.

Then came the itch. At first, it teased with a faint tickle beneath my skin, a subtle irritation creeping along unnoticed. Within moments, it surged, spreading in waves consuming every inch of my body. A thousand tiny legs crawled beneath the surface, moving in chaotic patterns I couldn't escape. My fingers raked across my arms, nails carved red streaks into pale skin. I scratched harder, more frantic with every second, as though tearing at myself might bring relief. Instead, the itch burrowed deeper, clawing into my flesh with an intensity leaving me trembling.

It crept across my chest, winding around my ribs, before snaking down my stomach and twisting along my legs. Each new movement unleashed fresh bursts of panic, crushing me beneath its relentless grip. The itch transformed into a blazing fire, burning through me, its heat stealing the air from my lungs. My breaths came in shallow, broken gasps, each one more desperate than the last. Relief never came. The torment dragged on, leaving me clawing at my own body, consumed by the inescapable need to make it stop.

My heart pounded out of rhythm, each beat slamming against my ribs with such force it threatened to tear my chest apart. The noise filled my head, drowning everything around me, until it became the singular sound hammering through my skull. My throat burned with every shallow breath, the muscles straining to pull in air, the atmosphere pressing down as though it carried weight. A bitter, metallic taste coated my tongue, clinging to the back of my throat. It carried the tang of blood and bile, a cruel reminder of every bad decision forced down before this moment.

When I tried to move, the world spun with violent intensity, a nauseating tilt sending me crashing back to the ground. My arms and legs jerked with spasms beyond my control, twitching as though my body no longer belonged to me. The rough pavement beneath me shifted and rippled, its jagged edges digging into my skin, serving as a cruel reminder of where I lay. I opened my mouth to scream, but no sound emerged, my voice trapped in my throat, crushed under the weight of everything wrong.

Broken flashes of the night before surged behind my eyes; fragments too distorted to piece together. Faces appeared and disappeared, their features melting into darkness. Laughter echoed in my ears, twisting into something sharp and menacing, merging with whispers closing in around me, suffocating and constant. "Get up," I told myself, but my legs refused to respond, twitching as the itch crawled across my back, spreading deeper through my nerves, as though it sought to devour me from within.

Time dissolved. I didn't know how long I lay there, trapped between the remains of reality and the nightmare pulling me to this place. Above me, the stars blurred into streaks of light, spinning in cruel, taunting patterns. Later, I learned the drug carried traces of Angel Dust, a revelation that should have jarred me awake, forcing me to take control. It didn't. Instead, I pretended I claimed a victory, a badge of honor to wear.

Silence wrapped around me after the high, heavy and suffocating. A pull dragged at the edges of my thoughts, forcing memories to resurface—images of who I once was and fragments of who I could become if I stopped running. Demons crouched in the shadows of my mind, daring me to face them. Redemption didn't crash into me. It flickered, fragile and unsteady, a dim light trying to break through the dark.

Nights stretched, swallowing time in their depths. Mornings pressed into me, a crushing weight I couldn't shake. The mirror reflected a stranger—a hollow face with darkened eyes, skin stretched over sharp bones. Pain radiated through my body, each movement dragging at my limbs, a punishment I couldn't escape. My mind swirled in a haze I built to keep reality away, but the questions cut through regardless. Can I keep living like this? How far would I push before everything shattered for good?

No singular moment saved me. No grand realization tore the cycle apart. Change crept in, each decision scraping away at the chaos I wrapped around myself. Drinking less became a matter of survival as my body rejected the poison. Drugs disappeared not in dramatic acts of willpower but through a quiet retreat, pulling back as I clawed toward anything less destructive to dull the pain.

The struggle tightened its grip, refusing to relent. Old habits wrapped around me, their allure impossible to ignore, pulling me back toward the false comfort of oblivion. Each day became a battlefield, the fight raging between the life I craved and the chaos I sought to leave behind. Addiction spoke in a voice I knew too well: Take another drink, another hit, and everything will make sense.

I chose sobriety, not with faith in ease or the hope of an ending to the fight, but because it became the last option for survival. Not for tomorrow or the promises of a better future—for the moment I faced right now.

I recognized the voice, its lies unraveling before me to expose the trap hidden beneath the comfort. It offered nothing beyond endless cycles of regret, the same hollow numbness consuming me for years. Some days, the temptation clawed at my resolve, sharp and unrelenting. The relief it promised lingered on the edge of my mind, tangible and inevitable. Each time I leaned toward surrender, mornings spent waking in strange places tore through my thoughts. Fear seized those memories, dragging me back to the moment my mother's trembling hands sifted through the wreckage I left behind. Her heartbreak filled the air, etched into the lines of her face, a pain she tried to mask with fragile strength.

Some days struck harder than others. Walking past a bar or catching the sharp tang of alcohol on someone's breath gripped my chest and sent tremors through my fingers. Memories surged forward—nights drowned in oblivion; mornings heavy with regret. The pull clawed at me, cold and relentless, halting me mid-step. I tightened my fists, forced air into my lungs, and braced myself against the ache. Surrender lurked close, a cost I refused to pay again.

Cravings tore at me, slicing into places already raw from the damage I left behind. Relationships lay shattered, trust frayed to threads, scattered across the ruins of my life. My parents stood among the wreckage, their faces lined with worry and disappointment as they tried to piece together the fragments of the daughter they once knew. My mother's trembling voice echoed through my thoughts. "Why won't you let us help you?" Her words pierced through me, though I turned away, unwilling to face their weight. Those memories refused to fade, digging deeper now, sharper than ever, clinging to the edges of my mind.

Rebuilding dragged at me with every step, each movement weighted as though I hauled a boulder uphill. Days bled into nights, the hours stretching endless and restless, loneliness wrapping around me in an unyielding grip. Grief surged through my chest in relentless waves, each one heavier than the last. Sleep brought no refuge, only nightmares—twisted scenes of the destruction I left behind, replaying on an endless loop. Progress crawled forward, slow and grueling, yet I pushed on. Piece by piece, I tore away the crutches I relied on—numbness, denial, and the lies I built to shield myself—and forced my body to move.

My parents became mirrors reflecting everything I shattered. Heartbreak etched itself into their faces, visible in every glance, a silent weight they carried without complaint. One night, my father's voice broke. "We want you back." His words hit hard, breaking through the walls I built to contain my guilt, forcing it to the surface where I couldn't ignore it. I unlocked the spaces I closed, letting their love pour in, their strength hold.

Temptation lingered, its whispers curling through my thoughts, offering relief I refused to believe. One drink, one escape, and everything will ease, it murmured. Those lies tugged at me, sharp and familiar. I pushed them away, forcing myself to remember waking in strange places, fear crawling through me as I pieced together hours lost to oblivion. My mother's trembling hands came to mind, cleaning the wreckage I left behind, her heartbreak etched into every quiet movement, no matter how much she tried to conceal it. That story no longer belonged to me.

This path unfolded in silence, offering no fanfare or triumph. Each day demanded a fight, a confrontation with guilt, and the resolve to move forward. The echoes of my past lingered, constant reminders of everything I endured. They hold no power over me. Instead, they measured the distance I crossed. My life remained imperfect, reclaimed with each step I took.

The uneven pavement pressed against my feet as I moved forward, each step tearing through the weight of guilt clawing at my chest. The echoes of my past chased me, whispering accusations in familiar voices. I clenched my fists, forcing my body to stay upright as the memories swirled. They pulled me toward a time when numbness shielded every nerve, but I refused to give in. Each whisper fell beneath my steps, pressed into the ground as I pushed forward on a path I carved through every mistake.

Days dragged, each one pressing harder against me, carving tension into my muscles and forcing emotions to the surface refusing to stay buried. Loneliness gripped my shoulders, pulling me into silence so dense it smothered every thought. Grief hammered against my chest, breaking through in relentless surges, tearing through my resolve and leaving fractures in its wake. Shadows gathered in the corners of my apartment, shifting with every movement, holding the weight of the past in their twisting forms. They didn't exist; they accused with every flicker, demanding acknowledgment.

The simplest actions transformed into battles. Sobriety turned every step into an uphill climb, each moment outside the grip of alcohol a victory I gripped with unyielding hands. Calling an old friend, spending a day without giving in to temptation—these moments became lifelines, pulling me back from the edge. Each breath stung my lungs when I woke clear-headed, proof this body still carried the strength to endure after everything it weathered. Those moments didn't push against addiction; they reclaimed the pieces of myself I once surrendered.

Some nights, silence pressed so hard against my ears it consumed everything else. Shadows crept closer, their whispers threading promises of escape, pulling me toward the void I once craved. Tremors surged through my body while I gripped the chair, fingers digging into the wood until my knuckles burned. The thought of drowning my pain loomed over me, heavy and dark, offering relief disguised as freedom. I stayed still, defying the pull of the familiar lie.

A knock broke the stillness, faint enough to vanish into the night. My heart jumped, confusion wrapping itself around hesitation while I pushed myself to stand. The door loomed in front of me, its cold handle brushing my fingertips when I reached for it. My thoughts screamed to retreat, urging me back to the fortress

I crafted from fear and isolation. Something deeper stirred—a quiet resolve driving me forward, steady and undeniable. The door creaked open, and I stepped into the unknown, ready to face what waited.

I pulled the door open, expecting a visitor, but my eyes locked on a folded letter resting on the floor. The edge caught the dim hallway light, casting a muted glow. My chest tightened as I crouched to pick it up, the paper thin and soft against my fingers. The handwriting stopped me, its familiar loops and curves sending warmth coursing through me. A name surged to the forefront of my mind—someone I did not speak to in years, someone I believed lost from my life forever.

My hands shook while I unfolded the letter, the faint rustle slicing through the silence and settling in the room as a fragile echo. The words stared back, bold and unwavering: *You're stronger than you think. I'm here if you need me.* My chest tightened, and tears blurred the ink as the message tore through walls I once believed unbreakable. The lines, hurried and raw, carried a weight far greater than their simplicity suggested. For the first time in years, someone saw me, and the shadow of being forgotten began to lift.

I pressed the letter against my chest, its weight anchoring me in unexpected ways. Memories surged—my mom gathering the broken pieces I left behind; my dad, grief carved into his expression. Friends who refused to walk away, holding onto the version of me they believed still existed. They deserved more than the hollow shell I became. They deserved the effort I denied them for so long.

The letter didn't erase my mistakes or offer salvation. Redemption murmured on the edges of my thoughts, its presence growing stronger with every step I took. Meetings and their rigid steps failed to resonate. My path stretched ahead; one I carved with my own hands. It has nothing to do with following someone else's rules. My way needed to hold meaning, built on something deeper than the rituals others relied on.

The weight of the bottle and the haze of the drugs no longer defined the fight. Sobriety demanded more than stepping away—it required stripping away every mask I created. Beneath layers of denial and distraction, the raw truth of who I became surfaced, undeniable and unrelenting.

Denial gripped me, digging into the edges of my mind. Pain churned beneath the surface, clawing for release, though I forced it deeper. I moved through each day with a mask so bound to my skin, impossible to remove. My body stopped numbing itself, but my mind clung to the lies I built. Every forced smile, every deflection, tightened the trap I created—a life I refused to endure anymore.

I stood in front of the mirror some nights, searching the reflection for answers. The hollow figure staring back carried unfamiliar features, a stranger shaped by choices I refused to confront. My identity fractured long ago, scattering pieces left behind questions without answers. Recovery never promised to undo the past or erase scars. It demanded standing in the ruins and forging something new from the wreckage.

A phrase echoed through my thoughts: *You're as sick as your secrets.* It lingered, not as a slogan or cliché, but as a truth cutting through the silence. Every buried memory clawed its way to the surface, demanding recognition. The shadows I avoided loomed closer, forcing me to confront them one by one.

Honesty rose before me, sharp and daunting, its jagged edges cutting through the illusions I clung to. No smooth road unfolded—a brutal climb over steep rocks and unforgiving terrain stretched ahead. I stood at the base, gripping the letter, its weight pressing into my palm as though it carried the burden of my entire past. This path belonged to me alone. The first step waited, and I would take it. No one else would lift me forward.

Dreams of my mom dragged me into restless nights. She sat across from me, her posture unwavering, hands resting in her lap. Her eyes radiated a warmth softening the sharp edges of the room, pulling me into a space quieting everything else. Words poured out of me—buried secrets and confessions of the mask I wore while everything inside fractured. My voice cracked with apologies; each one heavy with the weight of mistakes refusing to stay buried. She leaned closer, her arms wrapping around me, her presence steadying the storm raging inside, offering a silent promise of healing.

The dream broke apart too soon. Her lips moved, forming words carrying the promise of comfort, but the sound never came. Morning light tore through the illusion, harsh and unrelenting, stripping it away and leaving reality to press against my chest. Shame wrapped itself around me, a cold reminder her forgiveness existed within the confines of sleep. I clung to those moments, guarding them as treasures. They offered something absent in the waking world, a fleeting glimpse of redemption hovering beyond my grasp.

Outside those dreams, I ran from the truth. Each day, I moved through the motions of recovery, appearing where I needed to be while locking my real struggles behind an unyielding wall. Sobriety became a mask, a fragile shield hiding the turmoil boiling beneath the surface. I feared anyone noticing the ruin I carried, feared they might turn away without a second thought. Fear mirrored the rejection I inflicted on myself. I abandoned everything I used to be long ago; how did I expect anyone else to hold on?

Sunlight filtered through the trees in Central Park, painting restless patterns across the path. My steps slowed as I noticed her—a woman sitting cross-legged on the grass, her coat hanging loose over her bony shoulders. Her hollow eyes scanned the crowd, searching for something no one offered. The sight pulled me back to a version of myself I wanted to forget.

The ache of hunger surged in my memory, sharp and relentless. Cold nights on concrete, the gnawing emptiness twisting my insides until it blurred everything else. Survival stripped me down to desperation, and now, those echoes lingered, shaping every step I took.

I reached into my bag and pulled out an extra sandwich I grabbed earlier without knowing why. Now I understand. Her eyes locked on me as I approached, tension tightening her frail frame. I crouched a few feet away, keeping my voice low. "Here," I said, holding out the sandwich. "I've been where you are—hungry, sitting in the cold, trying to make it through the day."

Her fingers curled around the sandwich, shaking as she pulled it toward her. She unwrapped it, her movements deliberate, as though each one demanded effort. Her gaze flicked to mine, searching for something unspoken. Her voice broke the silence, raspy but unwavering.

"The hardest part isn't walking away from the drugs," she said. "It's figuring out how to live with yourself afterward."

Her words landed like a hammer, breaking through walls I thought impenetrable. Without the distractions I clung to, without the lies shielding me, what remained? The question settled deep, refusing to let go. Stripping everything away forced me to face scars and flaws I buried under layers of pretense. I didn't know if anything beneath it all deserved saving.

I nodded, more to myself than to her, as her words lodged deeper. Lies been my armor, wrapping me in false protection. Smiles became performances, excuses turned into rehearsed defenses, and I spent every moment convincing others—and myself—I had control. But her words stripped away the illusion, leaving nothing to cling to.

She didn't linger. She gave a slight nod, turning her attention back to the sandwich as though the moment between us never happened. I stayed crouched, watching her eat, the memory of my own hunger pressing against my chest. Her words didn't offer answers; they left clarity sharp and unavoidable. The life I pretended to lead became a cage, each bar built from denial and avoidance, locking me away from the truth I feared most.

I stood, brushing dirt from my hands, and let the weight of the moment settle. The breeze swept through the park, carrying the scent of leaves and the hum of distant voices. It wrapped around me, grounding me where I stood and what I carried. The storm within me didn't quiet—it roared, daring me to confront it. For the first time, I considered letting it.

The quiet hours of the night, the weight of my past pressed harder. Stillness exposed the cracks I tried to hide, pulling shame and fear into the open. The mask I wore fused to me, its presence suffocating. The fear of facing my reflection clawed at my chest, taunting me with the possibility I am too broken to repair. The ground beneath me crumbled, leaving no clear path forward.

In the darkness, something shifted, a faint spark pressing against the weight of fear. Tearing apart the lies loomed like an insurmountable task, though rebuilding demanded destruction first. Redemption would not arrive uninvited; it required dismantling every illusion I built to survive. Piece by piece, the facade needed to collapse before something unshakable emerged.

Dreams of my mom lingered, offering more than escape. Her presence carried a quiet strength, pointing me toward what I needed to uncover within myself. Redemption refused shortcuts or easy fixes. It demanded raw, unfiltered truth. Each jagged edge I buried and every scar I ignored waited for me to confront them.

Recovery offered no clean breaks or simple solutions. Moving forward requires reckoning with the past and navigating the pain coming with it. Each scar, every flaw, and all the choices leading me here demanded acceptance. This journey stretched beyond a single moment of clarity. It asked for relentless effort and an unyielding commitment to face the truth without turning away. The path stretched into shadows, undefined and daunting, a glimmer of possibility flickered at its edges. Step by deliberate step, truth by unflinching truth, I carved my way forward.

5

The Night Music Changed

Routine dragged me deeper, every night in the bar stripping another piece away. Cold glasses dug into my palms, their icy surface burning against my skin as liquor scorched a path through me, hollowing out everything it touched. The haze smothered the world, muting its edges until laughter and bright mornings fragmented into something unrecognizable. Those moments didn't vanish in an instant; they eroded over time, leaving behind the faint echo of a life slipping further out of reach.

A melody sliced through the bar, jagged and discordant, cutting past the low hum of voices and the sharp clash of glass against wood. Each note struck hard, forcing cracks I buried deep to rise to the surface. The air thickened with the stench of stale beer and sweat, clawing at my throat with every breath. Laughter, brittle and warped, grated against my ears, twisting into something harsh and unrecognizable.

The noise swelled, each beat driving deeper, tearing into my skull. Chairs scraped against the floor, their jagged screeches colliding with heavy footsteps pounding through the room, fracturing my thoughts. My body refused to move, as though the air itself thickened around me, trapping me in its grip. The bar exhaled decay, its walls sagging under the weight of unraveling lives, mine dissolving among them.

Fragmented features stared back from the mirror, blurred and distant, twisted into something unrecognizable. The face staring at me didn't belong to the person who laughed without hesitation or faced mornings unburdened by regret. My fingers tightened around the glass, its cold surface digging into my skin. The cracks stretched deeper, splintering both within and around me, holding my gaze as if daring me to look away.

I dropped into the unspoken spot at the bar, the stool carrying my presence night after night without question. Neon lights flickered above, scattering fractured reflections across the counter, their dim glow lost in the haze surrounding me. Slouched forward, I stared at the faint outline of a stranger in the surface, a version of myself I refused to recognize. Alcohol dulled my senses, and regret clawed at my shoulders, relentless and heavy. Conversations buzzed in the background, a low hum dissolving into static. Bartenders moved with practiced ease, sliding my usual drink across the counter—beer first, chased by whiskey, whatever sat closest.

The first sip numbed the edges of another wasted day, its chill spreading through me, unraveling the tension coiled deep inside. Whiskey followed, harsh and unrelenting, burning its way down and settling like a stone in my stomach. For a fleeting moment, the ache inside stilled, buried beneath the flood of alcohol. My fingers tightened around the glass, condensation pooling beneath my grip as I stared into the amber swirl, chasing answers refusing to emerge.

Memories surged, stubborn and uninvited. Laughter rang through my life, bold and untamed, carried by friends who turned every moment into something larger than life. Weekends unraveled into nights fueled by reckless energy, daring the world to stop us. Over time, those moments fractured, slipping away piece by piece, leaving behind silence, filling the void they abandoned. Faces I trusted faded into shadows, their departures carving cracks into everything I tried to hold together. Their laughter hovered at the edges of my mind, faint and unreachable, slipping further from my grasp with every passing day.

Life in the bar churned forward, indifferent to my presence. Chairs scraped against the floor, voices clashed in uneven waves, and glasses struck counters with dull, repetitive thuds. The air reeked of stale beer and sweat, its heaviness clinging to my lungs and making each breath harder. My grip tightened around the glass, its cold surface anchoring me. This place dismantled every piece of me, scattering fragments into something unrecognizable.

The bar consumed me, dim light flickering and shadows twisting along the walls. Music stabbed through the air, each note cutting deeper, refusing to relent. Voices blurred into the clink of glasses, hollow noise without meaning. This place trapped me, a mirror exposing every failure I failed to outrun.

Faces blurred as I stared into my drink, the amber liquid catching the light and mocking me with its shallow promise of relief. Strangers filled the room, but their laughter carried the weight of familiarity, each sound scraping against old wounds. A voice in the crowd triggered a memory—Sarah, her laughter once the backdrop to carefree nights, now reduced to an ache in my chest. Another figure, his silhouette jagged in my mind, echoed Jake's easy grin. Their absence burned, leaving nothing but hollow regret in its place.

I gripped the shot glass, its chill biting into my palm while heat clawed up my spine. Whiskey turned into my mortar and brick, forming walls I no longer knew how to break. Smoke curled through the room, thick and unyielding, twisting itself around my throat. The loneliness struck hard, deliberate, driving me deeper into the isolation I created.

I exhaled, air catching in my throat as I realized I drowned not in the drink but in the choices pulling me to this place. Each sip tore at the future I believed in, leaving behind jagged fragments impossible to rebuild. My fingers twitched against the glass, a fleeting urge to shatter it, as if breaking it might free me from the prison I built with such care.

Reality frayed at the edges, faces twisting into cruel reflections of my failures. Their laughter echoed from the past, warped by guilt and self-loathing. The question pressed down, heavy and unrelenting: Did I have the strength to claw my way back, or would I remain trapped in this haze? My chest tightened as I stared into the glass, its surface smooth and deceptive, revealing emptiness.

The amber liquid swirled in the glass, its reflections catching the dim light. Each drink stacked another barrier, locking me behind walls of my own making. Job offers I ignored flashed through my mind, friendships left to rot in silence. My hands tensed, a silent rage twisting through my chest, tightening around the space where purpose once lived. Choices weighed on me, heavy as stone, pressing against every breath.

Laughter snapped through the fog, cutting sharp and clear. Across the room, a group leaned together, their voices rising and falling with ease. Their energy burned, pulling my focus. My chest tightened as I gripped the glass harder, the contrast between their freedom and my silence unbearable. What would they notice first if I approached? A body slumped with defeat. A face marked by failure. The thought dragged my gaze downward, back into the drink, were safety drowned truth.

Music shifted, low notes vibrating through the air, heavy and relentless. The glass pressed into my palm, cold and unyielding, its weight anchoring me to this moment. The walls closed in, their presence sharp and suffocating, leaving no room to breathe. Tension coiled in my gut, a restless ache tearing through the silence I clung to. Each sip stripped away another layer, leaving jagged remnants impossible to reclaim.

The jukebox whirred in the corner, its song crackling to life. Noise filled the room, blanketing the gaps where silence dared to linger. The liquid in my glass rippled under the dim light, a false calm waiting to drag me under. My jaw clenched as the heat crawled up my neck. The drink promised escape, but the lie tasted bitter now.

The bar gripped me in its silence and noise, pulling me between movement and stillness. Change hovered waiting for me to take it or let it fall.

I grabbed the fifth shot—whiskey or vodka, I no longer cared. A twisting knot coiled deep in my gut, sharp and unrelenting. The glass hit the counter as the room spun, walls tilting, the floor threatening to vanish beneath me. Faces blurred and stretched, unrecognizable shapes floating in the haze. My chest pounded with a rhythm too fast, too harsh, each beat pressing harder. Sweat broke across my skin as nausea surged, raw and violent, rising without mercy.

I shoved myself upright, legs shaking beneath the weight as I stumbled toward the door. Voices murmured behind me, hands brushed my arm, but I pushed through, driven by the need to escape. Cold air slammed into me the moment I stumbled outside, the door crashing shut behind. The drop in temperature tore through me, forcing my lungs to pull in a jagged breath, heavy and strained.

Still, it wasn't enough.

I doubled over, my stomach twisting as dry heaves wracked my body. Muscles clenched, every gasp leaving me weaker. Bile surged, burning its way up, dragging something deeper with it. This wasn't alcohol alone, something buried and rotting tore free, clawing its way out. Acid scorched my throat, its sting dull compared to the crushing weight in my chest. Shadows crowded closer, tightening around me, their presence suffocating and unrelenting, sinking into my thoughts.

Each retch dragged me into a blackened void where memories twisted into grotesque forms. The bar dissolved, replaced by a maze of jagged walls echoing with mocking voices. Laughter ricocheted, sharp and familiar, belonging to people who walked away long ago. Faces flickered in the darkness, distorting into cruel masks, their grins sharp with contempt. They weren't here to help; they came to remind me of the poison I let consume me.

"You call this freedom?" A voice slithered through the haze, sharp and venomous. "You're trapped in chains you forged, every sip tightening your bonds."

Dim lights sputtered, collapsing into faint embers failing to push back the encroaching void. Music hammered through my skull, each pulse sharp and punishing, pulling me deeper into the abyss. I squeezed my eyes shut, but the images surged, vivid and unstoppable.

A party unraveled in my mind, vibrant and wild. Laughter cascaded around me, indulgence wrapped into every moment. The scene twisted, colors darkening into jagged, grotesque shades. Bottles crowded every surface, monuments to indulgence turned hollow. Cheers fractured into an oppressive hum, choking the air. Familiar faces melted into distorted masks, their eyes sharp with judgment, locking onto me without mercy. I slipped further, engulfed by fragments of something mimicking joy, shattered and unrecognizable.

"You're nothing without me," the voice growled, low and venomous. The shadow swelled, twisting and shifting with a rhythm defying reason. At first, it hinted at something human—a faint outline standing in the dim light. Its edges warped, limbs elongating into jagged lines, bending into impossible angles. Its head tilted, breaking the illusion of humanity altogether.

Two lights burned where eyes should be, heavy and unrelenting. They didn't shine; they consumed, pulling the darkness tighter around me. My chest locked as the shadow surged closer, its features emerging from the writhing void. The face took shape, distorted but familiar, dragging shards of recognition to the surface. Its expression tore through my mind, each detail clawing at the edges of memory.

The shadow invaded everything, not content to linger on the edges. It pressed into the air, filling my lungs, my thoughts. Each movement forced me deeper into its grip, cutting away the space I thought I had left to breathe.

It loomed closer, its jagged form writhing as if it struggled to stay contained. "I gave you purpose, Jess," it sneered, the voice shifting between a rasp and a roar. "Without me, you're lost. A shell. A nothing."

The realization pierced through me, cold and unrelenting, cutting deeper with every breath. This hangover didn't linger as an illusion; it lived, tangible and relentless, feeding on failures and choices ignored for too long. Its voice whispered before, offering hollow comfort in the shadows. Now, the creature's grotesque form twisted into focus, raw and consuming. My stomach churned as its shape shifted, arms splintering into writhing tendrils, clawing at the air, pulling everything into its suffocating void, erasing any chance of escape.

"I've always been with you," it hissed, its mouth twisting into a jagged grin. The teeth inside glinted, fractured pieces of glass catching the light. "Every drink. Every lie. Every time you ran instead of fought. I've grown because of you."

Cold dread pinned me in place as the creature leaned closer, its fiery eyes burning into mine. Breath caught in my chest; words strangled before they could form. Memories clawed their way forward—reckless nights, broken promises, mornings filled with regret. It followed me through them all, feeding on every failure, swelling with each mistake. My legs trembled, threatening to give out under the crushing weight, but its presence held me upright, refusing to release me, refusing to let me escape.

"You think you can fight me?" it taunted, laughter curling through the air like smoke. "You can't. You're mine. Always have been."

The darkness shifted, swirling with the creature's words, and the images burst into focus. My family appeared, their faces contorted with anguish, their eyes wide with silent pleas. My mother's hand extended toward me, tears streaking her face, glimmering under an unseen light. I reached for her, desperation tightening in my chest, but the shadow coiled tighter, yanking me back into its grip. Her light faded, swallowed by the creature's suffocating presence.

"You belong to me now," it growled, the words a final judgment. "Let go. Embrace the chaos, and you'll never feel anything again."

Something snapped inside me, a raw defiance cutting through the fear. My chest heaved as I gasped for air, and the world shifted again. The demon blurred, its form flickering as though it struggled to maintain control. Light seeped in at the edges of my vision, the faint glow of the city pulling me back.

The alleyway came into focus. My palm pressed against the damp brick, its cold solidity anchoring me to reality. The demon's shape wavered, shrinking back into the shadows, its laughter trailing off into silence. My legs gave out, and I slid to the ground, knees drawn to my chest. The cold bit into my skin, and the starless sky loomed above, vast and indifferent.

For the first time, the truth struck with unrelenting force, shattering every illusion of control. My body tensed, muscles locking under the strain, each breath scraping raw against my lungs. This night refused to blur into oblivion. Every part of me fractured, thoughts splintering, chest burning under a crushing weight pressing harder with each second. No escape remained, no path to outrun the reality closing in around me. Survival hung by a thread I already worn thin.

If I refused to stop, it threatened to devour everything. Air ripped through my throat in uneven bursts, my body trembling with every desperate attempt to hold itself together. Shadows twisted around me, spreading and tightening, choking away any sense of space or direction. The demon's voice slithered through my ears, its words clawing at buried failures and regrets, each syllable tearing fresh wounds open with brutal precision.

I locked my gaze on the black void, its depth stretching without end, pulling at me with an unseen force. The darkness crept closer, pressing in and cutting off every direction. My mind twisted under the demon's words, its voice tightening around me, each syllable carving deeper into the cracks I tried to ignore.

"You think you can resist me?" it spat, its tone dripping with mockery. "You've built me with every failure. Every broken promise, every time you reached for the easy way out, I grew stronger because of you. And now, you dare to stand here as if you've got a fight left?"

The shadows around me shifted, pulsating with its venomous words. "You want freedom? Freedom is struggle. Freedom is pain. And we both know you've never had the strength for that."

Its laughter reverberated through the void, cutting and sharp, digging into places I didn't want to confront. "You'll stay here. You always do. Stop pretending, you're nothing. Let the emptiness take you. It's what you want, isn't it? To stop pretending, to stop trying."

The space around me closed in further, the void encasing me in its relentless pull. Images surfaced in my mind—every mistake, every misstep, and every excuse used to avoid responsibility. The demon's voice fed on them, weaving them into an undeniable truth.

A flicker stirred deep inside. Defiance. Fragile, undeniable, but present. The void stretched vast, growing stronger with every choice I allowed it to consume. This moment demanded action, the chance to reclaim something before it all vanished. Hesitation risked everything. The only option left was to fight.

The demon hissed, its form shifting with agitation. "You can't win. You never do. Give in. Stop this pointless struggle and let the darkness finish what you started."

My hands pressed against rough brick, fingers scraping over cold, unyielding stone as I steadied myself. The void pulled back, its tendrils retreating into the darkness, but its presence hung close, poised to strike at the first sign of weakness.

I scanned the empty space, the quiet oppressive, the faint hum of the city beyond struggling to pierce the haze clouding my thoughts. No shadows writhed; no voice whispered in my ears. The demon withdrew, but its presence clung to the edges of my awareness, coiled and waited, feeding on hesitation and fear.

The ground didn't swallow me, and I refused to fall. My legs trembled, muscles strained, hands raw from the fight to remain upright. Still, I stood. A thought broke through the haze, fragile and persistent. The darkness circled close, pressing in, but it didn't take me. Cold air bit into my skin as I inhaled, sharp. Not tonight, I thought.

I sat motionless, unsure how much time slipped away, until a faint sound broke through—the music. Carried on the wind from the bar's jukebox, it reached me, distant but persistent. A slow, mournful melody drifted through the air, slicing through the haze clouding my thoughts. It tugged at memories I thought I buried, mornings when I woke sober, when hope still had a place in my life, when I believed in something beyond the empty promise of the next drink.

A flicker stirred deep inside, different from the numbness weighing me down. Fear crept in, sharp and unfamiliar, whispering, I might have fallen too far, the hole I dug too deep to escape. Another feeling followed, harder to name. Maybe hope, maybe desperation. Whatever it was, it stirred enough to make me shift, to consider standing, to imagine moving forward.

The shadows in the alley writhed, stretching and shifting, living tendrils reaching for me. Their movement grew heavier, darker, pressing closer, as if they could taste the doubt and fear coursing through me. A cold sensation slid down my neck, a breath brushing against my skin. The whispers weren't voices but sensations—pulling, urging, tempting. Each flicker of movement clawed at my resolve, sending tremors of panic rippling through my body.

For years, I thought the darkness had been my refuge, a shield from the pain, a place to hide when the weight of living became too much. Every bottle I opened, every night I spent adrift in oblivion, fed the shadow lurking within. Now it stood before me, not as a haze or a figment, but as a predator. Its hunger grew with each reckless choice, its presence undeniable, its intent suffocating.

Sweat slid down my spine as realization struck—this wasn't a companion or a comfort. It wanted more than my moments of weakness; it wanted everything. My soul. The pit in my stomach deepened, the instinct I ignored for years roaring to life. The shadow was no ally; it waited, poised for the moment I would falter. Shame surged alongside the fear, the heat rushing to my face as the truth took hold. I been its prey all along, feeding it with every misstep, every denial. The weight of that knowledge coiled in my chest, heavy and unrelenting.

I stumbled back, pressing against the wall as its rough surface anchored me in place. Night buzzed with unnatural energy, alive in a way setting my nerves on edge. Faint laughter drifted from the bar, distant echoes reminding me of what I walked away from, what I abandoned for the solace of the bottle.

Promises of oblivion whispered, tugging at the corners of my resolve. Relief closing, but the cost loomed larger than I could afford. Control slipped through my fingers long ago, and now the rules changed.

Darkness pushed closer, feeding on my hesitation, its presence heavy and insidious. Whispers wove through the air, each word a blade urging surrender, while phantom claws scraping at my skin, threatening to drag me into a pit where no light could reach. Shadows coiled tighter, swirling like smoke around my ankles. Each movement carried an unnatural weight, testing my resolve with every flicker. Panic surged, sharp and electric, as a single question surfaced: what if I let it win? A shiver cut through me, and the image of being swallowed whole. The void didn't threaten, it waited, patient and hungry, its intent unrelenting.

Faces of those who disappeared into the same darkness flashed in my mind—friends reduced to hollow versions of themselves, their eyes empty, their presence nothing more than shadows of who they once were. That same fate loomed over me, close enough to taste. Images of my family rose unbidden, their confusion and pain pressing against me, heavy and unavoidable. Disappointment hung in their expressions, cutting deeper than any blade. They didn't understand the choices that led me here, the path I had carved through drink and despair. Aching, as brutal as it was, felt less damning than the grasping shadows.

A jolt of desperation shot through me, a frantic need to run, to move, to escape. No clear path appeared, only the suffocating reach of the darkness encasing every corner of my mind. Each shadow carried the weight of my failures, dragging my choices into sharp focus. The demon's face emerged from the void, a grotesque distortion of everything I feared. Its grin stretched wider, daring me to take the final step and surrender.

I pushed off the wall, my legs trembling beneath me but moving forward. The faint melody from the bar's jukebox found me again, different now—steadier, stronger. The sound cut through the noise in my mind, weaving through the shadows clawing at me, daring me to collapse. A voice in the music, soft but insistent, called to the part of me that hadn't let go.

"You don't want this," I whispered to myself, forcing the words past the tightness in my throat. My steps faltered, but I kept moving. The darkness surged, its weight pressing harder, as though it could sense the shift inside me. The demon's voice snarled, venomous and sharp.

"You can't outrun me, Jessica. You'll fail, like you always do. This fight doesn't belong to you. Stop pretending."

The shadows swirled, growing denser, but the music swelled too, its notes more vibrant, more alive. Each step I took felt like breaking through chains, like tearing free of something gripping me for years. The demon hissed, its whispers turning to shouts, a barrage of every failure I'd buried, every regret I tried to drown. My breathing grew unsteady, the weight inside me rising, threatening to choke out the momentum I fought so hard to build.

But the music didn't falter. Its rhythm grew steadier, louder, a pulse matching my steps. The melody reminded me of mornings I forgotten—the warmth of the sun on my face, the quiet moments when I still believed I could find my way back.

"Not tonight," I said, the words trembling but firm. The shadows lashed out, trying to pull me back, but I pushed harder, each step forcing them to retreat. The demon's laughter rose, desperate, clawing for control.

"You'll come back," it hissed. "You always do."

The bar's lights appeared ahead, dim but steady, cutting through the alley's oppressive darkness. The music wrapped around me like armor, shielding me from the voice holding me captive for too long. The shadows thinned, the void retreating as I moved forward, step by step, toward the light.

"No," I whispered, forcing the word out as if it could anchor me. "You won't win." The promise carried weight, unfamiliar but necessary. Shadows edged closer, their presence thick, pressing against the spark I refused to let die.

Move. Escape. The demon's presence loomed, suffocating and relentless, I knew the real battle wasn't with it—it was with me. My hand gripped the wall, rough stone biting into my palm as I steadied myself. Running wouldn't save me. The darkness demanded confrontation, a reckoning with truths I buried for too long. Teeth clenched, I pushed away from the wall and took the first step forward.

My legs wavered, trembling under the strain, each movement unsteady but determined. The wall provided balance, I kept moving, each step driving me closer to the sidewalk. The cool air hit my skin, sharp and grounding, clearing the haze enough for thought to break through.

Returning to the bar meant slipping into the same pattern, drowning the fear and emptiness in poison. I convinced myself alcohol equaled salvation. That path promised ease, comfort, but I knew its end. I walked it too many times, always finding the same emptiness waiting at its conclusion.

Or I could walk away.

My body dragged with exhaustion, muscles resisting every movement. I turned from the bar, breaking the poison's hold. Each step forward clawed at me, slow and heavy, but I didn't stop. No destination lay ahead, the need to leave behind the prison driving me forward. The road stretched before me, empty and open, and freedom hovered out of reach, close enough to chase.

By the time I reached my apartment, my head throbbed, and my eyes threatened to close with every step. The keys slipped from my trembling hands, clattering against the floor. The metallic clink echoed through the hallway, each sound a sharp reminder of my unsteady grip on reality. Wrestling with the lock dragged into a torturous battle, each second stretching. The door opened, and I stumbled inside, collapsing on the couch, too drained to make it to bed. Every muscle screamed, my stomach churned, but I remained. Breathing. Alive.

Pale light pushed through the blinds, casting sharp lines across the room. The wreckage of my living room came into focus—empty bottles littering the floor, crumpled wrappers piling on the table, every object a remnant of nights surrendered to the dark. I pressed my face into the cushions, desperate to silence the whispers clawing at the edges of my thoughts. The bar lingered nearby, its pull undeniable, promising the same hollow escape. The temptation coiled around me, taunting with false relief. My stomach churned, revulsion slicing through the fog clouding my mind. I clenched my fists, forcing the urge down. Not this time.

Morning arrived like a hammer to my skull, each pulse of pain relentless and unforgiving. My mouth carried the sour sting of stale alcohol and regret, a bitter reminder of the choices that led me here. I pushed myself upright, nausea tearing through me, threatening to pull me under again. The bottle sat within reach, its presence as tempting as ever. My hand hovered but didn't fall into the familiar habit. Not today. Instead, I reached for a piece of dry toast, forcing it down alongside water tasting sharper than I remembered. A small act, defiant and necessary, a step away from the demon's grip.

Cravings struck over the next few days, each one crashing harder than the last. There were moments I faltered when the pull of the bar seemed too strong to resist. Shadows lingered at the edges of my mind, flickering and shifting, their whispers promising escape, their presence suffocating. Every breath carried the memory of how simple it been to drown everything out, to trade chaos for the fleeting silence a drink brings.

The siren calls of the past came alive with cruel clarity, the phantom clinking of glasses, the low hum of voices, the haze wrapping around me like armor. The demons fed on those memories, their voices louder, more insistent, clawing for the control I refused to give.

I replayed that night in my mind, the way my body screamed for relief, the way the music shifted into something sharper, more deliberate. Each beat pounded in my chest, driving home how close I stood to the edge. The weight of my choices crushed down on me, as though the walls of my apartment sought to close in. Shadows lingered, circling like predators, waiting to pull me back toward the bar and its false comforts.

I didn't turn to rehab. I avoided counseling. The thought of sitting in a room with strangers, trading confessions, turned my stomach. Instead, I chose isolation. I cut ties with those who fed my spiral, distancing myself from the people who shared their problems over drinks. Bars became off-limits, their empty promises something I refused to chase anymore. My days no longer belonged to bottles and hollow conversations. Each step forward cut into me, raw and unfamiliar. Progress dragged, every movement a battle, but I pressed on. Control slipped through my fingers for too long, and I refused to lose it again.

I spent more nights alone, the silence pressing in like a suffocating weight. Darkness crept closer in those quiet hours, threatening to choke the resolve I clung to. Sleep offered no escape—dreams turned into battlegrounds where I faced shadowy figures with twisted smiles and taunting voices. Each night became a war, a brutal clash between the pull of the bottle and the fragile spark of hope daring to fight back. I woke drenched in sweat, heart pounding, the echo of laughter lingering in my mind like a cruel reminder of the nights I lost, the times I surrendered.

The struggle tested me in ways I hadn't imagined. Temptation came in whispers, urging me to reach for my phone, to text an old friend, to suggest grabbing a drink. My hand hovered over the screen more times than I wanted to admit, but I stopped myself every time, forcing the phone away.

To keep the shadows at bay, I searched for new ways to fill the empty hours. I walked for miles, letting the crisp air clear my thoughts and the sun's warmth remind me of life beyond the darkness. Books became my refuge. I immersed myself in stories, vivid worlds pulling me from my own, for a little while.

Still, the cravings refused to vanish. They lingered in the background, quiet but ever-present. I caught myself standing in front of the refrigerator, staring at the empty space where bottles once lined the shelves. The ache in my chest whispered of the numbness I left behind, the way it dulled the pain. But something new begun to stir within me—clarity. For the first time in years, my thoughts weren't clouded, and the world outside my window looked sharper, more alive.

As I stood there, watching the world move beyond my small space, a flicker of something unexpected surfaced: hope. It wasn't loud or commanding, but it refused to fade. I clung to it, knowing it was fragile, knowing it could shatter with a single misstep. For the first time, I believed in its persistence.

Each small victory brought me closer to breaking the chains I forged around myself. My demons still hovered, waiting for me to stumble, and I knew the fight wasn't over. It never would be.

6

Lost and Found

I struggled to understand why it took a demon—a nightmare made real—to force me to recovery. Not the friendships I destroyed, not the years I wasted, not even the mornings spent staring at a stranger in the mirror had pushed me to this point. It took something dark and relentless, a physical embodiment of fear, to cut through the fog. Its cold stare pierced through every wall I built, stripping away the layers I used to hide and leaving me more exposed than ever before.

Walking through the city streets, I couldn't shake the sense that something inside me changed. My thoughts circled back to that encounter, prodding it like a raw wound, testing if it still ached. The demon itself wasn't the focus. Its presence represented something far more—a final warning, or perhaps a wake-up call delivered too late. For years, I existed in shadows, retreating to dark corners of my mind where regrets and fears festered. Shadows, though, don't stay still; they deepen. That night, they swallowed everything.

A voice whispered in my mind, relentless and cruel: "Why didn't the people you hurt matter enough?"

The question struck like a blade, sharp and unanswerable. My mother's disappointed eyes surfaced in my thoughts, her calls fading as I pulled further away. Memories of friends surfaced too, the ones who tried to guide me toward something better, a flicker of light, a chance at stability. They had reached for me, only to step back when I shut them out, again and again. None of it been enough to force a change. Every sign, every warning, I ignored, convincing myself I could outrun the truth.

Under the pale city lights, I wandered without purpose, a hollowness settling deep inside. The streets lay quiet, broken by the occasional laugh from an alley or the distant hum of a passing car. Around me, the city seemed tense, holding its secrets close. How many others carried burdens no one could see, battles fought in silence but powerful enough to define them?

That night with the demon wasn't a battle. It stood motionless, its presence rooting me in place, making escape impossible. I didn't care what it wanted; I wanted to get away. But running didn't matter. It mirrored everything I'd buried, every truth I ignored. Seeing it left no escape. I couldn't turn back, couldn't forget what it revealed.

I leaned against the lamppost, the cool metal firm beneath my grip. A siren cut through the silence, a reminder of how fragile everything can be. I moved through life, avoiding conflict, skimming the surface without purpose. Each day blurred into the next, leaving me hollow and lost in repetition.

The demon forced me to confront truths I buried. Its presence went beyond a single night, marking the turning point I couldn't ignore. Hiding in the darkness, clinging to the illusion of safety, held nothing for me. The lie crumbled, leaving me exposed with no escape.

Storming out of my house replayed in my mind—the slammed door, the defiance, the belief that I needed no one. The memory struck like an open wound, fresh and raw.

Ahead, a neon sign flickered over a diner, casting uneven light across the street. Drawn to its glow, I walked inside and slid into a booth. My gaze fell to the chipped table as the waitress approached, pouring coffee without a word. Her tired eyes offered a quiet understanding before she walked away, leaving me to face the thoughts I had avoided for too long.

I sat in the corner of the diner, the bitter aroma of brewed coffee mingling with the sweet scent of pastries, creating an atmosphere comforting and homey. My hands cradled a steaming mug, its warmth a welcome contrast to the chill of the autumn air seeping through the window. I watched people bustle past, their laughter and chatter a stark reminder of the connections I severed. Outside, life flowed like a river, vibrant and full of possibilities, while I remained anchored to my table, the coffee steaming in front of me like a lifeline. As I took my first sip, letting the warmth spread through me, I was caught in the throes of memory.

People who had reached out over the years surfaced in my thoughts, those who saw something in me worth saving. One by one, I let them slip away, until nothing remained but an empty life and a city humming with a thousand forgotten dreams.

Why did it take so long to see the truth? The question cut through me, raw and unrelenting. Denial built walls around me, each choice to ignore reality adding another layer. My thoughts returned to a night that should have shattered everything, a moment impossible to ignore. Instead, I buried it, turning away and letting it fester in the cracks.

Steam curled from the coffee in my hands, warming my skin but failing to ease the chaos inside. Memories surfaced, sharp and insistent, clawing for space.

One stood out above the rest. I sat in a car that wasn't mine, streetlights streaking across cracked vinyl seats and unfamiliar faces. Voices filled the air, laughter and shouts rising over music that rattled the windows and shook the entire car. My shoulders pressed into the seat, a futile effort to feel part of something reckless, daring, alive.

I wanted that spark, something real to hold onto. Instead, unease twisted in my stomach, tightening with every cheer and every shout. The thrill around me rang hollow, the shadows deepening, watching, daring me to admit I didn't belong.

Laughter spilled from my mouth as I let the bravado pull me under. I shouted with the others, the pounding bass rattling my chest. Outside, the city smeared past in streaks of light and shadow, blurring into a restless stream of concrete and neon. I told myself this was freedom—raw, fast, untouchable.

The cracked vinyl seat pressed against my back as the music thundered through the car, shaking the air around us. Streetlights stretched into long streaks, melting together as the speed picked up. I wanted to believe I was part of it, that their boldness could rub off on me, pulling me into the rush they all seemed to feel. My laugh sounded hollow, trying to drown out the faint pull of nerves twisting my chest. Something felt wrong, though I couldn't place it.

Kevin's hands gripped the wheel, his knuckles glaring white against the dark leather. His gaze flicked between the road ahead and the rearview mirror, tension sharpening every movement. The slow approach of headlights caught my eye, the police car inching closer, its beams slicing through the dim interior, scattering shadows across uneasy faces.

The steering wheel creaked under the pressure of Kevin's hold. His jaw tightened, the moment pressing down like a storm gathering force. The light from the police car swept through the cabin, glinting off tense features, the silence growing heavier with each passing second.

"Stay cool, man," Luis said, leaning back in the passenger seat. His grin carried an edge that unsettled more than reassured. "I changed the plates, remember? They've got nothing on us."

Changed the plates? The truth hit hard—this car wasn't ours. Stolen. Not a reckless joyride, but something darker, something that could ruin everything.

The weight inside the car pressed down, dense and choking. My hand hovered near the door handle, instincts urging me to flee while my body remained frozen, paralyzed by the shock of what I learned. They lied, concealing the truth, knowing I never would have stepped into this trap if I'd known.

Cop car lights strobed through the cabin, painting Kevin's face in shifting shadows. His grip crushed the wheel, every movement rigid and deliberate as his focus alternated between the mirror and the road. Tension radiated from him, heavy and unspoken, swallowing the false bravado filling the car moments earlier. Silence grew oppressive, stretching with each passing second.

Adrenaline surged, burning through me, twisting into dread that clung to every thought. My gaze locked on the door, fingers inching toward the handle, but my body wouldn't follow through. The realization trapped me, weighing down every decision, every breath.

The cop car turned down a side street, leaving the glow of its lights behind. Inside, the tension broke like a dam, laughter bursting from Luis as he clapped Kevin's shoulder. The car filled with triumphant voices, their celebration rising in stark contrast to the panic still coursing through me.

"They didn't suspect anything," Luis said, his grin stretching too wide. "Easy."

The sound of their cheers hung in the air, grating against every nerve.

A brittle laugh escaped me, forced and unnatural, as panic tightened its grip. The world around me blurred, every sound and movement distant, as though I'd been yanked from my own body. Promises of freedom and fun twisted into something darker, something I hadn't agreed to.

Streets narrowed as we veered deeper into unfamiliar territory, the graffiti on the walls sharper, more hostile. The city's edges turned jagged, and the buildings seemed to lean closer, crowding the car. Every crack in the road jolted through the frame, sharp shocks refusing to let me sink into denial. Escape churned in my thoughts, but every option felt impossible. Kevin and Luis thrived in this chaos, feeding off an energy I couldn't share. The realization burned through me, each second heavier, pinning me in place with nowhere to turn.

Laughter swelled inside the car, louder than the thudding music shaking the seats. A plastic bag crinkled as it passed between them, its contents shifting—small packets of white powder mixed with loose joints. Kevin and Luis traded grins and jokes, their excitement crackling like static. The bag stopped in front of me, daring me to join. My fingers hovered, caught between reaching and retreating, every instinct at war. Take it, and everything might quiet for a moment. Refuse, and risk their judgment, their questions. My hand stayed motionless, gripped by indecision, while their eyes lingered, waiting for me to choose.

Fingers trembling, I reached for the joint, aware of their eyes on me. Kevin nudged my arm, his grin sharp, daring. "Come on, Jess. Don't freeze up. Live a little," he urged, the words heavy with expectation. The air hung thick with the pungent blend of weed and cocaine, saturating my senses with every breath. I lit the joint, dragging in smoke that scraped against my throat and coated my tongue with bitterness. A fleeting haze dulled the edges of my panic, but the unease clung to me, unshakable. My hand lowered, the joint pinched between my fingers as my gaze shifted toward the girl sitting beside me. She leaned closer, her knee brushing against mine, her movements languid but purposeful. Dark hair tumbled over her shoulders, catching the light in strands of gold. Her lips curved in a faint, teasing smile, but her eyes told another story—sharp, watchful, filled with something electric that stirred under my skin. I swallowed hard, heat creeping up my neck as her presence pulled me into the moment.

Luis leaned over the seat, the plastic bag crinkling in his hands. "Your turn," he said, his voice low and full of amusement. His finger dipped into the bag, emerging with a streak of white powder pressed into his nail. He held it out to her, his grin cocky as he waited. She didn't hesitate, leaning forward to sniff the cocaine from his nail with practiced ease. Her hair brushed my arm, soft and warm, and the scent of her faint perfume mingled with the acrid air around us. My breath hitched, the closeness stirring something I hadn't felt in years. She leaned back, her head tilting toward me as she laughed, the sound rich and smooth. "You don't know what you're missing," she murmured, her voice low enough that only I could hear. Her knee pressed against mine, the contact sending a jolt through me that I tried to ignore.

Luis passed the bag to Kevin, who took his share without missing a beat, but my attention stayed fixed on her. She tilted her head, watching me as if waiting for a response, her lips curved in that same faint, knowing smile. The chaotic energy in the car swelled around us—Kevin's laughter, Luis's jokes—but it all faded under her gaze.

The car slowed, the uneven streets outside blurring into a grim palette of cracked pavement and shadows. My hand tightened around the joint, the smoke curling upward, the smell clinging to my clothes and hair. The girl shifted beside me, her shoulder brushing mine, and my pulse quickened. Her presence felt intoxicating, as dangerous and alluring as everything else in this car. I glanced at the door, the handle just within reach. My fingers itched to grab it, to push the door open and step into the heavy night air. Her voice lingered in my ear, soft but insistent, making me question whether I wanted to leave or if I was just too scared to stay.

Kevin eased the wheel, his movements deliberate, but his grin widened as he glanced at the rearview mirror. Luis leaned back, wiping his nose with the back of his hand before twisting around to glance at me. "You good, Jess?" he asked, his voice casual but laced with something sharper, a challenge that hung in the air.

I forced myself to nod, the motion stiff, my grip tightening around the joint. The girl beside me shifted again, her head tilting as she studied me. "You sure?" she asked, her voice low, the teasing edge gone, replaced by something quieter, more curious.

We finally came to a stop in a rundown part of the Bronx, the engine rumbling softly as Kevin parked near a cluster of rundown buildings. Graffiti-covered walls stretched upward, their faded colors blending into the cracked pavement below. The heat inside the car felt oppressive, and my lungs ached for fresh air.

Luis opened his door first, stepping out with an exaggerated stretch, his movements loose and full of swagger. "Let's go," he said, motioning for the rest of us to follow. Kevin climbed out next, slamming the driver's side door before glancing at me with a raised eyebrow. "You coming or are you just going to sit there?" he asked, his tone dripping with mockery.

I hesitated, my hand still hovering near the door handle. The girl beside me moved first, her knee brushing mine as she slid out of the car with effortless grace. Her hand rested on the edge of the doorframe, and she glanced back at me, her dark eyes locking onto mine. "Let's go, Jess," she said, her voice carrying a strange warmth that made my chest tighten.

I stepped out into the humid night, the asphalt radiating the heat of the day. The city felt alive in a way that wasn't comforting—its sounds too sharp, its shadows too deep. Luis and Kevin were already ahead, their voices cutting through the stillness as they joked and laughed, their energy unrelenting.

The girl lingered near me, "They'll leave you behind if you wait too long," she said, her lips curving into that faint, knowing smile.

"I'm not going with them," I said, my voice low but steady. The decision planted itself as I turned, moving in the opposite direction. My steps were slow at first, my legs stiff and unsteady, but with each stride, my pace grew firmer. The sounds of their voices faded into the distance behind me.

"What the fuck, Jessica!" Kevin's voice ripped through the air, sharp and furious, slamming into my back like a physical blow. "Where do you think you're going?" His anger reverberated; a volatile force I could feel growing stronger.

The slam of a car door jolted through me. His footsteps pounded against the pavement, heavy and fast, closing the distance between us. His voice, slurred and raw, chased me, his rage biting at my heels.

I kept moving. My breath came in sharp bursts as I pushed forward, refusing to turn around, refusing to stop. The street stretched ahead, unfamiliar and unwelcoming, but I walked into it anyway. Whatever waited for me in the darkness, it couldn't be worse than what I was leaving behind.

Voices rose behind me, sharp and cutting, their tone dripping with mockery. Every step widened the gap between me and their noise, but their voices refused to fade. "You're too fucking high to be out here alone!" she shouted, her tone straddling irritation and worry. Her words clung to the air, but I didn't turn back. "Seriously, you think you're invincible or something. This ain't the place to play brave."

Luis's voice broke through next, casual but sharp enough to cut. "She thinks she's better than us now, huh?" The sound of his chuckle followed, low and grating, carrying that same dismissiveness he always wore like armor. "Go on, Jess, but don't think you can come crawling back."

Laughter cracked behind me, jagged and loud. Kevin's sneer cut through the noise; his words slurred but unmistakable. "Fuck that dyke!" The venom in his tone clawed at my back. "Her pussy ain't shit anyway!" His laughter rose again, raw and unfiltered, mingling with Luis's quieter snickers.

My fists clenched as the insults pressed harder against me, each word searing through the distance I created. My legs carried me forward, each step forcing the noise behind me to blur into the night. Their derision lingered, heavy but not enough to make me go back.

The girl's voice pierced the laughter, "Jess..." There was no anger this time, just something softer, almost fragile. "Don't go like this." Her tone lingered, curling into the space between us.

Luis's chuckle drifted closer, mingling with Kevin's sneering tone. I felt their eyes on me, felt the lingering judgment in every moment I kept walking. The pull to turn around battled with my resolve to keep moving, but I didn't stop. Each step widened the gap between me and the mess I was leaving behind.

Breath tore through me, each inhale sharp, as the world tilted. Blurred streets and streaks of neon dissolved into shadows, heat pressing heavy against me. Their laughter followed, sharp and biting, echoing as if branding my failures.

Desperate to break free, to prove their mockery wrong but no sound emerged, my mistakes sealing my voice. Each step widened the distance from the night I escaped, from the people I once considered friends. Their laughter faded into the background, while shame clung to me, pressing heavier with every stride. Something fractured within me, raw and unnamed, as though a part of me dissolved in the wreckage I allowed to take hold. I fled from more than them—I fled from the version of myself shaped by their world.

The city dragged me into its restless streets, its energy overwhelming and uncaring. For weeks, I wandered without direction, seeking shelter wherever the night permitted. Park benches, the shadows of sprawling trees, and the steel gates of shuttered storefronts became temporary refuges. Each place hollowed me further, stripping away any sense of belonging as I moved through the days, fading into the city's ceaseless rhythm. Darkness stretched without end, each night dissolving into the next. Isolation became my refuge as I buried myself in the city's constant motion, avoiding the wreckage. Shame clawed at me, consuming every fleeting thought of reaching out. The streets became an escape, pulling me deeper into their distractions. I surrendered to them, convincing myself that disappearing into their noise offered more relief than trying to rebuild what lay in ruins. I learned to find comfort in the city's rhythms, the late-night bustle of delivery trucks, the laughter of strangers spilling out of clubs, and the occasional blare of a siren in the distance. Life moved on around me, unbothered by the girl clinging to her fractured sense of self. Hunger became a familiar ache.

Desperation coursed through me, raw and unrelenting, sending shivers through my limbs. My body felt brittle, my thoughts fractured, teetering on the brink of something I couldn't escape.

Pavement stretched beneath my feet, scattered with cigarette butts and broken glass catching the glare of streetlights. I lingered near the curb, trying to stand tall, forcing confidence that didn't exist. A man walked by his face worn and unyielding. My gaze caught his for a moment, a silent plea etched across my features. He glanced at me, read my desperation, and walked on without hesitation. I cursed under my breath, bitterness clinging to my tongue as my stomach clenched with hunger. My hand tightened around the crumpled bills in my pocket, a meager offering begged by strangers earlier in the day. Not enough for food, but enough for something to quiet the ache, to dull the shame pressing in on every side. The thought of getting high turned my stomach, but the relentless ache twisted deeper. A car sped by its bass pounding through the air, shaking my resolve with every heavy beat. My gaze drifted to the other women on the corner, their tired faces telling stories I couldn't ignore.

I'd become one of them. A girl trading pieces of herself for survival, numbing the pain to keep the darkness from devouring her. As a child, I'd watched women like this through the car window as my mother drove us through the city. Their glassy eyes and frail forms stirred pity in me then, along with a promise: I would never let life break me that way. Here I stood, lips trembling as I forced a smile, knees buckling under the crushing weight of my own downfall.

A couple of guys approached, laughing and shoving each other as they swaggered down the street. One of them caught my eye, his gaze narrowing, lingering as he took me in. "What's up?" he drawled, his tone slow and laced with mockery. "Looking for a good time?"

My lips twitched into a smile, brittle and fake, shattering halfway before it could hold. "Depends," I forced out, my voice thin, a hollow attempt at flirtation. "What are you offering?"

He moved closer, the sharp stench of cheap cologne curling into the air between us, turning my stomach. "Damn, girl," he laughed, "you look like you've seen better days."

His friend nudged him, glancing at me with a mixture of pity and dismissal. "Leave her, man. She's strung out."

Shame flared, burning against my skin as I straightened, words spilling out before I could stop them. "I'm fine," I snapped, though my voice wavered, betraying the lie. "I just need—" The sentence collapsed; the truth too fractured to finish. Food? Sleep? A hit? The needs tangled, indistinguishable, leaving me hollow.

Their laughter trailed behind them as they walked away, leaving me alone in the noise of the street. My knees gave out, sending me sliding down the wall until I hit the pavement. My hands trembled as I wiped at my face, smearing tears with the grime of the city. The sobs came hard and ugly, echoing in the narrow alleyway. Knees pulled to my chest, I let my head fall forward as memories clawed their way to the surface.

My mother's voice filtered through the noise, soft but worn. "We're better than that, honey. We have a future." That promise felt cruel now, a distant hope shattered somewhere along the way. All that remained was this broken version of me—begging, grasping, selling away dignity piece by piece just to survive another day.

Every fear I had growing up, every promise I made to myself, lay in ruins. The city around me moved on, relentless and indifferent, its energy brushing past my collapse like I wasn't even there.

My gaze caught on a small rental office wedged between a laundromat and a boarded-up deli. The grimy window and flickering neon sign didn't inspire hope, but it offered one thing I hadn't known in years: a chance to stop running. I scraped together enough money for a room, holding onto that transaction as if it could somehow pull me out of the wreckage. The room barely held together. Walls stained yellow peeled at the edges, and stale air pressed heavy around me. The single window rattled in its frame, failing to muffle the relentless noise from the street below. The space carried the weight of years, its fragile state mirroring my own, teetering on the brink of collapse. It belonged to me. For the first time in weeks, I could sit without bracing for someone to push me along or force me to move. Leaning my head against the uneven wall, I let exhaustion take over, no longer fighting to keep myself upright. The cracks in the paint drew my attention, small imperfections branching out like veins across the surface. I told myself this room could be a beginning, the first step toward reclaiming something I'd thought lost. Not much, but it existed.

Peace remained elusive. The building's thin walls offered no barrier to the chaos outside. At night, muffled arguments seeped in from neighboring rooms, voices climbing in anger or breaking with desperation. Bottles clinked together, their brittle sound of people numbing themselves in cheap liquor. Sometimes there was laughter, loud and strained, or the sound of quiet sobbing echoing down the narrow hallway. Each noise clawed at my frayed nerves, a relentless reminder that even here, I was surrounded by brokenness. A fragile sanctuary, hanging by a thread, threatening to collapse from everything it tried to hold back.

I spent most nights on the sagging mattress, staring at the cracked ceiling, every bump in the springs digging into my back. Sleep was a cruel stranger, arriving in fragments too short to provide rest. I woke to every creak or crash from the world outside, heart pounding, the darkness pressing in from all sides. Even here, alone in my room, I couldn't escape the suffocating feeling of losing myself. A part of me wanted to believe I could climb out of this, find something real and stable again. Each night, as the city raged outside my window, that fragile hope dimmed, slipping further from reach.

One afternoon, as I wandered through the streets, a hand gripped my arm. I spun around to see an older man standing in front of me. Deep lines marked his face, and his steady gaze didn't waver. Without a word, he pushed a flyer into my hand.

"Security training," he said, his tone firm. "It's free, and if you finish, they'll get you a job."

I looked down at the flyer. Bold letters read: *Free Security Training. Employment Guaranteed.* Doubt curled as I moved to hand it back, shaking my head.

"You don't believe me," he said, holding his ground. "I've been where you are, thinking there's no way out. This program helped me. It can help you too. You don't have to keep living like this. You deserve more than the streets."

His words lingered. I hesitated. "Why are you doing this?"

"Because someone did it for me," he said, his voice unwavering. "Take the chance. They'll help you if you let them."

He turned and walked away, disappearing into the crowd before I could say another word. I stared at the flyer in my hand, the corners rough against my skin. My first thought, to toss it, let it fall to the pavement like everything else. Instead, I folded it and tucked it into my pocket. Maybe it wouldn't change anything, but for some reason, I couldn't throw it away.

It all came together on an otherwise forgettable Tuesday. I found myself sitting under the harsh flicker of fluorescent lights in a room filled with strangers. The instructor droned on, their words blurring into static as my mind wandered. Then I noticed her—Esther. Her laughter broke through the monotony like sunlight cutting through heavy clouds, drawing my attention in a way nothing had for months. She sat a few seats ahead, her presence magnetic, pulling me out of my fog. When her eyes met mine, the air shifted, and for the first time in what felt like forever, a flicker of hope sparked within me.

Esther stayed in my mind, a quiet pull I couldn't ignore. When class ended, I lingered near the doorway, caught between the urge to approach her and the fear of being dismissed. I forced myself forward, my words awkward but sincere as I introduced myself. Her smile met me with warmth, easing the tension. The conversation unfolded naturally, her presence grounding me in a way I hadn't expected.

The classroom buzzed with restless energy, the instructor's voice droning through a list of protocols and procedures. My body sagged with exhaustion, the hunger gnawing at me making it impossible to focus. Every shift in my seat reminded me of the discomfort, but I stayed, willing myself not to slip into the fog creeping at my awareness.

Esther's voice drew my attention again. Her laughter, rich and unrestrained, cut through the dull monotony of the room. She leaned toward a classmate, her ease with others something I couldn't help but notice. Her energy softened the sterile environment, offering a moment of clarity. When her eyes met mine, her expression shifted. Concern replaced the laughter, her gaze locking on me as if she saw through every layer I tried to hide behind.

After class, I gripped my backpack tightly, standing motionless in the hallway. My instincts screamed to leave, to avoid risking rejection, but something held me there. Esther walked toward me; her steps purposeful. She stopped beside me, her presence steady as if waiting for me to speak first.

"Hey," she said, her voice gentle but firm. "You, okay?"

I forced a smile, but it felt brittle. "Yeah, just tired," I replied, hoping the lie would sound convincing.

Esther didn't seem convinced. She studied me, her eyes narrowing, she could see straight through the cracks I was trying so hard to patch up. "You sure?" she pressed. "You look like you haven't slept in days."

I sighed, the exhaustion creeping into my voice. "It's... been a rough couple of weeks," I admitted, my defenses crumbling. "I'm just trying to get my life back on track, you know?"

Her expression softened, and she took a step closer, lowering her voice so that only I could hear. "Listen, I know it's none of my business, but if you need a place to crash, even for a night or two, I've got an extra room. No strings attached."

The offer, a lifeline, but I couldn't believe it. I blinked at her, stunned by the unexpected kindness. "Are you serious?" I asked, my voice cracking.

Esther nodded. "Completely serious. I've been where you are," she said, her eyes full of understanding. "Sometimes, a little stability makes all the difference."

Before I could respond, the instructor's voice called us back for the next session, and the moment was interrupted. Esther reached out and touched my arm. "Think about it, okay?" she said, her smile warm and genuine.

I nodded, swallowing hard. "I will," I promised.

When I asked Esther about renting her extra room, she answered without hesitation. "Of course," she said, her tone steady, as though the decision already been made. Her certainty left me stunned.

A week later, I stood at her door with my battered bookbag slung over my shoulder, carrying everything I owned.

"Hey," Esther greeted, her smile wide and welcoming. The soft apartment light highlighted her pixie cut, the sharp edges of the shaved sides blending into loose curls that framed her face. "You made it. Need a hand with that?"

I shook my head, gripping the straps of my bag tighter. "No, I've got it," I said, my voice faltering. "Just... taking it all in, I guess."

Her gaze lingered, calm and steady, before she motioned toward the hallway. "Come on, let me show you your room."

Following her through the narrow hallway, I counted each step, my chest tightening with a mix of nerves and gratitude. She stopped at a door with chipped paint and pushed it open. The room was small but safe: a bed with a worn quilt folded at the foot, a sturdy wooden dresser, and a window filtering in soft, golden light.

I set my Jansport on the bed, fingers brushing over the faded quilt. "Thank you," I said, turning to meet her eyes. "I don't even know how to express it enough but thank you."

Leaning against the doorframe, "It's not much," Esther said, watching my reaction. "It's yours now, I hope it gives you some peace. A place to start over. To breathe."

Her words settled over me, breaking through some of the weight I carried. I allowed myself to believe starting over could be real. I swallowed back the rising lump in my throat, the sting of tears blurring my vision. "It's perfect," I whispered. "Thank you, really. I don't know how to repay you."

Esther still leaning against the doorframe, her smile softening. "You don't owe me anything. You know," she added, her voice taking on a reflective tone, "someone did this for me once, when I was lost and didn't know where to turn. I promised myself that if I ever saw someone in need, I'd pay it forward. This is me keeping that promise."

"I've been on my own for so long," I confessed, my voice cracking. "It feels strange... having someone care."

Esther's eyes met mine, full of genuine empathy. "We all need someone," she said, her voice quiet but unwavering. "Even when we think we're better off alone, remember that."

"So, what's the house rule?" I asked, trying to lighten the mood.

Esther's eyes lit up with mischief. "Rule number one: no eating my leftover pizza. Rule number two: you have to try and beat me at board games at least once a week."

I laughed, the sound foreign to my ears but welcome. "Deal," I agreed, feeling a weight lift off my chest.

Just then, Angie's voice floated in from the living room. "Esther! Are you torturing our new roommate with those rules already?"

Angie appeared in the hallway; arms crossed in mock seriousness but her eyes shining with warmth.

"Jessica, this is Angie, my partner," Esther introduced, her grin widening, rolling her eyes. "Angie is the real enforcer around here," she whispered. "Don't let her fool you."

"Don't listen to her," she said, raising an eyebrow. "I'm fair. Just don't leave the dishes unwashed for more than a day, or you'll hear about it."

I nodded, the easy banter between them made me feel more at ease. "Got it. No leftover pizza stealing and no dirty dishes. Anything else?"

Angie gave me a quick once-over, then smiled. "Welcome," she said, her voice kind. "Don't let Esther fool you with all her rules. We're pretty laid-back."

I managed a shaky smile, the casual banter between them easing some of the tension coiled inside me. "I think I can manage that."

The two of them exchanged a look, and for a moment, the air felt lighter, easier. Angie reached out, patting my shoulder. "We'll all get used to each other," she said. "Take it one day at a time."

I nodded, my heart feeling a little less heavy. I felt like I might belong somewhere. Esther's eyes met mine, filled with a quiet hope that mirrored my own.

"Welcome home," she said.

And for the first time in what felt like forever, I believed it.

Esther's apartment gave me space to breathe. The air hummed with quiet moments—shared meals, soft music, and conversations that lasted late into the night. Esther and Angie welcomed me without hesitation, their kindness steady and unspoken, letting me find my footing one day at a time.

I staggered through the door, gripping my throbbing head as withdrawal tore through me. Cold sweat clung to my skin, and my stomach churned with relentless knots. Heat seeped through the windows, but it did nothing to stop the tremors racking my body.

I scrubbed my face with cold water earlier, hoping to pull myself together, but every muscle clenched, caught in a vice.

Esther sat cross-legged on the living room floor, flipping through a stack of old vinyl records. "Hey," Esther greeted, looking up with a smile, though her eyes narrowed with concern as she took in my pale complexion and the tremble in my hands. "You look like you've been through it. You, okay?"

I let out a weak chuckle, dropping my bag by the door. "Yeah, just... getting used to this sober thing, I guess."

Esther set the record she was holding aside and got to her feet, brushing her hands on her jeans as she approached me. "It'll get better," she said, placing a gentle hand on my shoulder. "I know it doesn't feel like it now, but it will."

I nodded, grateful for her kindness, even though the hope she offered felt far away. As I lowered myself onto the couch, Esther glanced toward the kitchen. "Want some water or tea?" she asked. "You should stay hydrated."

"Water, please," I croaked, my throat dry and raw.

As Esther disappeared into the kitchen, Angie, her partner, poked her head into the room. Her short, dark hair tied back, and her eyes were warm and welcoming as always. "Hey, Jess," Angie greeted, wiping her hands on a dish towel. "How you holding up today?"

I managed to smile. "Getting there."

Angie's brow furrowed, and she stepped closer, her voice gentle but firm. "You need anything? Seriously, don't try to tough it out alone."

Tears stung my eyes, unbidden and embarrassed. I bit my lip, trying to keep my composure. "I just... I feel like a mess," I admitted, my voice cracking. "I don't want to be a burden."

Angie sat down beside me, the couch dipping under her weight. "Hey," she said, her voice full of warmth, "you're not a burden. We've all been through rough patches. It's okay to lean on people who care."

Esther returned, handing me a glass of water. "Here," she said, sitting on the armrest beside me. "Drink up, and then we'll take it slow. Maybe get some fresh air later if you're up for it."

I sipped the water, my hand shaking so bad I needed to grip the glass with both hands. The cool liquid soothed my parched throat, but my stomach still twisted with unease. Esther and Angie exchanged a glance, one that spoke of quiet understanding, and I knew they were worried.

Angie leaned forward, her eyes searching mine. "You've got this, Jess. We'll be here every step of the way, okay?"

Esther sensed the turmoil brewing inside me. She leaned in, her voice dropping to a whisper. "I know you're struggling, but you're not alone, okay? We'll get through this."

I took a shaky breath, my tears spilling over. Angie placed a hand over mine, and Esther squeezed my shoulder. In that moment, surrounded by their kindness and unwavering support, my heart began to beat.

Settling into this new chapter, I couldn't help watching the way Esther and Angie moved through life together. Their connection unfolded in small moments—tender glances, shared laughter, a steady rhythm of mutual care. It stirred something deep within me, a quiet longing for that same kind of intimacy and understanding. Their presence pulled me back to memories I hadn't revisited in years, memories of middle school and the girl who changed everything.

Kathy stood at the heart of those years. Her hair caught the light in wild, brown-golden streaks, matching her uncontainable spirit. She dominated the football field with confidence demanding attention, tackling boys twice her size and proving herself fearless. From the sidelines, I watched her in awe, feeling both drawn to and apart from her world. She moved through life, pulling people into her orbit with a laugh that seemed to chase away shadows.

Though I never joined her on the field, the moments we shared away from the games stayed with me. Those afternoons, full of laughter and unguarded conversations, grounded me in a way I hadn't known I needed. Often an outsider, I watched as Kathy's confidence and kindness reached out to everyone around her, and somehow, she always made sure to include me. Her presence held an unspoken warmth, her laughter a steady light that broke through even my darkest doubts.

In Esther and Angie's home, Kathy's memory lingered, tugging at the edges of my thoughts. Her friendship offered more than a fleeting connection; it opened a door to parts of myself I hadn't faced. I never told her how much she mattered, but the way she brought light into my life left a mark I could never erase.

Watching Esther and Angie, I saw the power of belonging in unexpected places. Connections with Kathy, Melissa, and now Esther and Angie grounded me in a world I once believed to be unstable. Recovery is not about discarding the past—it is about finding strength in those who reached out when I couldn't stand on my own. Each friendship became a step toward piecing my life back together.

With those thoughts swirling, I decided to reach out to Kathy. Her unwavering support had always stayed with me, inspiring me to embrace my truth. One evening, I sat on the couch, the warm glow of a lamp spilling across the room. My phone rested in my hands, and I hesitated, my thumb hovering over the screen. Would she remember the moments we shared? The shy smiles during recess? My chest tightened as I typed the message.

Hey Kathy, it's been a while! I've been thinking about our middle school days and wanted to tell you something. I had a crush on you back then. I never had the courage to say it, but you were always so special to me. I'm glad we've stayed friends.

The seconds stretched as I waited for her reply, my pulse pounding in my ears. When the notification chimed, relief washed over me.

Wow, I remember those days! You were always so sweet to me. I'm glad you told me. It means a lot to hear that from you. I always thought you were amazing!

Reading her words, my secret lifted. It was liberating to express my feelings, to acknowledge that crush from years ago. Our friendship and bond stood resilient against time.

I glanced toward the kitchen, where Esther and Angie laughed as they teased each other over a half-finished meal. Their joy radiated warmth, pulling me into the moment. They reminded me that life was about sharing, about finding happiness in the ordinary.

As I leaned back into the couch, a smile spread across my face. The past no longer held me captive. I could embrace who I was, speak my truth, and open myself to the relationships that would shape my future. This wasn't just survival anymore—it was a beginning....

The bell above the diner's door jingled, pulling me from my thoughts. My hands wrapped around the ceramic mug, its warmth anchoring me. Conversations blended with the soft clinking of silverware, a rhythm that cut through the quiet hum of fluorescent lights above.

Rain-slick streets gleamed through the window, neon signs casting fractured colors in puddles scattered along the sidewalk.

New York had sharpened my edges, but it was in Esther and Angie's apartment that I rediscovered something I'd lost: a sense of belonging. Their space, small but filled with understanding, became a haven I hadn't thought possible.

I raised the mug, letting the heat seep into me. Their kindness hadn't just offered shelter; it planted something within me—a quiet hope I couldn't ignore. The shadows of the past still lingered, and the road forward promised no guarantees, yet the connections I'd forged gave me strength to keep moving. The city stretched beyond the glass, restless and alive. Its reflection reminded me that while the journey continued, each step mattered.

7

Masks and Mirrors

A crooked mirror clung to the wall; its tarnished frame chipped at the edges. Cracks stretched across the glass, splintering my reflection into uneven fragments. Fingers gripped the cold porcelain sink, grounding me as I stared into eyes burdened by truths left unsaid.

The bathroom light flickered overhead, uneven and harsh, casting jagged shadows across my face. At 35, my life resembled a borrowed script, a narrative dictated by others rather than shaped by my own choices. Years of rehearsed moments and forced smiles hollowed me out, burying the truth beneath layers of pretense that no longer served me.

Water poured from the faucet, the rush filling the small space. Steam curled upward, vanishing before it could linger. My gaze fixed on the stream, the distance between who I am and who I've become stretching beyond reach. Maybe it started when I first understood my truth clashed with everything I'd been taught. Or maybe it began with realizing my version of love existed outside their rules.

I cupped water in my hands and splashed it onto my face. Droplets clung to my skin, refusing to slide away, echoing the shadows of the past etched in my thoughts. Washing it away didn't change anything—it remained, a weight pressing from every side.

The reflection in the mirror revealed a face I recognized but couldn't claim as my own. A scar cut through the skin above one brow, cheekbones remained sharp, and a mouth sat silent, closed against words it had forgotten how to form. The features stood there, defiant, familiar but distant.

A vibration jolted through the quiet, pulling my attention to the phone on the counter. My stomach knotted as I reached for it, wishing to see Melissa's name glowing on the screen. She had a way of appearing when I began to fall apart, her voice steadying everything that threatened to slip away. Instead, an unimportant notification blinked back at me, another hollow echo of a world I could no longer touch.

Setting the phone aside, I dried my hands and stepped into the bedroom. Faint evening light crept through the blinds, painting slanted patterns across tangled sheets on an unmade bed. Rest had become elusive; stolen by thoughts I couldn't quiet. I sank onto the edge of the mattress, hands dragging through my hair as memories clawed their way back to the surface again.

As a teenager, I would lie awake, the darkness closing in as my mind raced. In gym class, I watched the other girls whispering about boys, passing notes scrawled with hearts and names, their voices full of excitement. I envied their ease, their certainty. My gaze drifted to the girls themselves—the way their eyes lit up, the curve of their smiles. What they felt for boys, I felt for them. I used to think something was wrong with me. I used to think I was broken. I sighed, closing my eyes, letting the darkness settle around me.

The first time I told anyone, it was Melissa. We were at Nash Park, sitting on the swings. The chains creaked with every gentle sway, the sound louder than my own voice. My hands gripped the cool metal tightly, my pulse thrumming as I tried to push the words out.

"Mel," I began, staring at the worn sneakers scuffing the dirt beneath me. "I need to tell you something."

Melissa froze mid-swing, her gaze snapping to mine. For a moment, the silence felt unbearable, but then her lips curved into a grin, wide and teasing. "Yeah, no kidding," she said, giving me a playful shove. "I've been waiting for you to figure it out."

Her ease, her humor, made the weight I carried shift, lighter somehow. "You're not... weirded out?" I asked.

"Jess, you're my best friend. I don't care who you like. Just don't crush on me—it'd be awkward," she teased, winking. Her laugh rang out, warm and familiar, and I found myself laughing too, relief bubbling up in a way I hadn't expected. I wasn't carrying the secret alone.

Melissa was the first person I trusted with the truth for so long. We were twenty, sitting at Tick Tock Diner sharing a greasy meal late at night after hanging out at the clubs. She dipped a fry into a pool of ketchup, her eyes narrowing at my fidgeting hands.

"What's going on with you?" she asked, popping the fry into her mouth. "You've been weird all night."

I stared down at my half-eaten burger, my appetite long gone. My stomach twisted, the words fighting to come out. "I think I am going to tell my family."

She leaned forward, suddenly serious. "Are you ready?"

Her question hung between us, sharp and unrelenting. "I don't know," I admitted, my voice barely audible over the low hum of the diner. "What if they hate me for it?"

Melissa's expression softened, but her voice remained firm. "Jess, you've been carrying this for years. I've seen what it's doing to you. You deserve to stop hiding."

I let out a shaky breath, my fingers tightening around the edge of the table. "It's not that simple. What if they don't understand?"

"They love you," she said, her tone steady. "And if they don't get it at first, you'll make them understand. It's your truth. They can't take that from you."

I nodded, but doubt gnawed at me. The idea of baring that part of myself to them felt impossible. "Once I say it, I can't take it back."

Melissa smirked, leaning back in the booth. "You don't want to take it back. Trust me. Keeping it in? That's what screws you up. You deserve to live your life without all this...weight. Without the fake relationships."

I nodded, the knot in my stomach tightening. "I think I'm scared of everything changing."

"Change isn't always bad," she said, grabbing another fry. "Sometimes, it's what saves you. And anyway, I'll be here now stop with the 'woe is me' crap. You're gay, big deal. It's about time you started owning it." She shoved the fry in her mouth. "Now eat your food."

Melissa made it sound so simple, so natural, and for a while, I let myself believe it could be. "Thanks, Mel. I don't know what I'd do without you."

She grinned, lifting her soda as if to toast. "Good thing you'll never have to find out."

Ten years passed before I worked up the courage to tell my family. I rehearsed it a hundred times, imagining every reaction—anger, disappointment, rejection—but nothing could prepare me for sitting at the dinner table, their expectant eyes on me.

The words felt foreign as I spoke to them. "I'm gay."

My dad blinked, his brow furrowing as he processed the words. My mom set her fork down, her expression unreadable. For a moment, I thought I'd made the worst mistake of my life. Then she reached across the table, her hand warm as it covered mine. "We know, Jess," she said, her voice soft. "I've always known."

My breath caught, the weight of her words both a relief and a revelation. "You have?"

"Jessica, I'm your mother. Of course I know."

I turned to my father, whose brow furrowed as he glanced between us. "Well," he said after a long pause, clearing his throat, "I suppose I should've seen that coming."

The laugh that escaped me was watery and half-sobbed, but it was real. "You're not mad?"

"Mad?" He shook his head, patting my shoulder. "You're still you. That's what matters. I'm proud of you for being honest."

My mom shook her head. "Never. All we want is for you to be happy."

It wasn't perfect—there were questions, moments of awkwardness—but it was more than I had hoped for. Years of fear and doubt dissolved as I sat there, surrounded by a family that hadn't turned away. They didn't have all the answers, but they were willing to try. They stayed, and that was all I needed.

Pain and confusion from my past still surfaced, leaking through the cracks that coming out hadn't sealed. They lingered like shadows. The abusive relationships I survived marked me, but what infuriated me more was the way people tried to connect those scars to my queerness. They saw trauma as the root, claiming my identity was something I turned to, not something I always carried.

I crossed the room to the window, pressing my forehead against the glass, its cool surface grounding me. Outside, streetlights blinked to life, spilling yellow pools onto the pavement. Headlights carved through the twilight as cars rolled by, distant and unimportant. The scene felt removed, as if I were watching it through a fog.

Relationships flickered through my mind, both the ones that burned bright and the ones leaving me scorched. Women who made me feel alive, their presence electric and undeniable, contrasted with men I'd been with out of obligation. Those memories surfaced like sharp edges, cutting through the veil of time. I remembered the nausea following those encounters with men, how I'd rush to the shower, scrubbing my skin until it stung, desperate to rid myself of the wrongness.

Recklessness defined those years. I threw myself into moments without care for consequences, searching for something fitting, something that made sense. I gravitated toward unavailable women, their lives knotted with complications. Married women, mothers, those seeking the same escape I craved. Our entanglements offered fleeting connections but left more questions than answers.

And then there was her.

I closed my eyes, leaning harder into the glass, memories struck without warning, sharp and vivid. She was strength and fire, a mother who loved with an intensity that made me believe we could create something lasting. For a while, I thought we had. Until it unraveled.

When it ended, I shattered. Nights blurred into a haze of substances and chaos, every reckless choice pushing me further from myself. No one could fill the void inside me, no matter how much I tried to escape into them. The climb back from that darkness wasn't quick or clean, but it was mine.

I turned from the window to face the mirror, locking eyes with the woman staring back. This wasn't about masks anymore. The layers I used to hide behind had fallen away, leaving nothing but the truth of who I was. My reflection didn't scare me like it used to. It wasn't perfect, but it didn't have to be.

The city outside buzzed with life, its rhythm a reminder that the world kept moving. For the first time, I wasn't fighting against it—I was moving with it. The person in the mirror wasn't a shadow of someone else's expectations. She was me.

No need to pretend anymore.

The memory of her still lingered, a quiet ache that I carried longer than I cared to admit. Love wasn't the problem—it was never the problem. The problem was me, or maybe timing, or the weight of our separate lives pulling us apart. Whatever it was, the ending left a scar that I hadn't managed to smooth over.

And then Christine stepped into my life.

It wasn't planned, wasn't something I went looking for. If anything, I was still avoiding love, keeping it at arm's length, too afraid to let anyone get close enough to leave another mark. We met by chance, a gathering neither of us wanted to attend. Mutual friends, cheap beer, and a room full of strangers milling around. The kind of event where mismatched chairs lined the walls, and folding tables were covered with homemade crafts and baked goods. It wasn't my scene, and I lingered near the exit, ready to leave as soon as I could justify it. I'd been standing in the corner, sipping something lukewarm, when I saw her.

She stood near a table of secondhand books, her fingers skimming over the spines with an easy grace. Something about her caught my attention—the way her dirty blond hair fell into her eyes, the soft curve of her smile as she picked up a book and read the back cover. She had a presence, a quiet confidence that made the room smaller, less overwhelming.

Our eyes met from across the room, and for the first time in a long while, I felt myself lean into the moment instead of shrinking away but I talked myself out of it. I told myself not to approach her. She probably wouldn't notice me, and if she did, what would I even say? When I turned to leave, I bumped into someone, sending their drink sloshing over the edge of a paper cup.

"Whoa!" a voice said, rich with amusement. "Careful there."

It was her.

I froze, my words tangling somewhere between my brain and my mouth. She smiled, holding the drink steady, and for a moment, the world narrowed to just the two of us.

"Sorry," I managed, my voice small.

"Don't worry about it," she said, her tone easy and forgiving. "It's just cider."

She introduced herself and before I knew it, we were talking—the books she'd picked up, how neither of us really wanted to be there but had shown up anyway. Conversation with her felt natural, as if we'd known each other for years instead of minutes. When she laughed, it was unguarded, the kind of sound that settled something restless inside me.

By the end of the event, I'd worked up the nerve to ask for her number. To my surprise, she handed me her phone before I even finished the question, her smile soft but sure.

"Here," she said. "Text me sometime. Maybe we can grab coffee."

And I did.

We'd been texting ever since. Nothing serious, just light exchanges that somehow carried more weight than I wanted to admit. Each message from her was a small spark, lighting up the parts of me I thought long since dimmed.

My phone buzzed; it *was* her.

Coffee this weekend?

I smiled, unable to help it, my heart skipping a beat at the simple message. She didn't know it, but she'd become the highlight of my week, the one thing making everything feel a little less heavy. I typed back quick, my fingers moving faster than my mind.

Saturday, 11?

Her reply came instant: *Perfect. Can't wait.*

My chest tightens with a mixture of excitement and fear. I wanted this. I wanted her. But what if this ended up like the others? What if I messed it up like I always did?

I shook my head, trying to push the doubts away. This time was different. I wasn't hiding anymore. I wasn't pretending to be someone else. For the first time, I was walking into something as me. All of me.

Saturday arrived, my nerves trailing me like shadows. The coffee shop smelled of fresh espresso and warm pastries, the air heavy with the comfort of routine. Christine sat by the window, her hair catching the sunlight like threads of gold. Her smile met me before her words did, and the tension in my chest loosened its grip.

"Hey," I said, sliding into the seat across from her.

"Hey yourself," she replied, her voice warm, her eyes holding mine. "You look... happy."

I laughed, feeling the blush creep up my neck. "I am. Now that I'm here."

We ordered our drinks, and as we talked, everything else faded into the background. The sound of the espresso machine, the chatter of other customers—it all became a distant hum, like white noise. I focused on her, on the way her lips moved when she spoke, the way her eyes lit up when she laughed. The way she made me feel like I didn't have to hide any part of myself.

As we talked, I found myself letting go. The usual walls I built to keep people out seemed unnecessary here. Christine didn't ask for the polished version of me. She seemed content with who I was, cracks and all.

"I'm glad you asked me out," I admitted, my voice quieter than I intended but no less honest.

She leaned in, her smile soft but certain. "I'm glad you said yes. I've wanted to do this for a while."

I bit my lip, trying to contain the smile that threatened to spread across my face. There it was—the possibility I'd been hoping for, the beginning of something real. And I didn't feel afraid. Christine didn't know it, but she had become the reason my days felt lighter, the person who made me believe there could be more than just surviving.

I reached for my cup, our fingers brushing, sending a spark through me. This was the start of something beautiful. Something that didn't require masks or mirrors.

8

Through the Storm

It's funny how the mind can turn on you. One minute, you're okay functioning, smiling, pretending like everything is fine. And the next, you're spiraling, drowning in a sea of emotions you can't control or understand. Today was one of those days. The anxiety had crept up slowly, like a predator stalking its prey, waiting for the perfect moment to strike. And when it did, it hit me hard.

The walls of my apartment felt like they were closing in on me. The familiar hum of city life outside had faded into the background, barely perceptible against the rising tide of panic swelling inside my chest. My breaths were shallow, quick, and uneven. My hands shook as I gripped the edges of the kitchen counter, trying to ground myself in the present moment. But it wasn't working. Not today.

I closed my eyes, trying to focus on my breathing like the therapist had taught me. *In through the nose. Hold. Out through the mouth.* I counted each breath, but the tightness in my chest only seemed to grow. My thoughts were racing, a tangled mess of fears and doubts that wouldn't quiet down.

What if I never feel better? What if this is my life forever?

The thought alone was enough to send a fresh wave of panic crashing over me, and I clutched the counter tighter, my knuckles turning white.

The truth is this wasn't new to me. I've been here before. Too many times to count. This dark place, this suffocating weight that wrapped itself around my chest and refused to let go. Anxiety had been my companion for as long as I could remember, whispering lies in my ear, telling me I wasn't good enough, that I was broken, that I'd never be happy.

I opened my eyes and stared out the window at the city beyond. It was a beautiful day, the sun shining brightly in the clear blue sky. But all I could feel was the storm raging inside me, blocking everything else. I wondered if anyone walking by on the street could see if they could sense the turmoil churning just beneath the surface. Or if I was as good at hiding it as I thought I was.

It wasn't always like this. There were good days, too—days when the weight lifted, when I could breathe without feeling like I was suffocating. Days when I could laugh and mean it, when the future didn't seem so bleak. But on days like today, it felt like the bad outweighed the good.

I knew I needed to pull myself out of it. I couldn't stay in this place, trapped in my own head, letting the fear and doubt consume me. But knowing that and doing it were two very different things. It's hard to fight a battle when the enemy is inside your own mind.

Some days, it feels like my brain is constantly at war with itself. I'll wake up, and the sunlight will pour through the blinds, gentle and warm. But it doesn't reach me. It never quite does. The light hovers, taunting me with the idea that today could be different, could be better—but the weight in my chest always tells me otherwise.

Anxiety is this shadow that never fully leaves. It lingers, even in moments of quiet. It tells me to worry, to overthink, to doubt everything I'm doing. And then there's the depression, an anchor pulling me deeper whenever I try to stay afloat. Together, they're like echoes in my mind—loud, constant, and inescapable.

I've battled them for as long as I can remember, but no matter how hard I fight, they always come back. They're there in silence, in the noise, in the spaces between every breath I take. Sometimes I wonder how long I can keep fighting, but I remind myself that I've made it this far. That's something, right?

There was a time when I didn't understand any of it. In my teens, I thought maybe I was just broken, that I couldn't be fixed. I never told anyone back then because, honestly, how do you explain a sadness that doesn't have a reason? How do you explain anxiety when nothing is technically wrong?

Over the years, I've had plenty of people tell me to "just be positive," as if that was the magic solution to everything. They don't get it. Staying positive isn't just a choice I can make. It's a fight, every single day. Some days, I can fake it. Other days, like today, I'm barely holding it together.

I take a deep breath, trying to shake off the fog. I know I should call someone, maybe reach out to one of my friends, but the thought feels exhausting. Even just texting can feel like climbing a mountain sometimes.

Still, I will try. I must try.

I pull out my phone, my fingers hesitating over the screen. I don't need to tell them everything—I've gotten pretty good at pretending everything's fine. But maybe, just maybe, talking to someone will help break through this. I send a quick text to one of my friends, just a simple "Hey, how are you?" It's easier to ask about them, to focus on something outside of myself for a minute.

While I wait for a reply, I stare out the window, watching the world go on without me. The trees sway gently, the neighbors laugh in the distance, and life moves forward, whether I'm a part of it or not. Some days, that thought scares me. Other days, it brings a weird kind of comfort. It's like the world doesn't need me to keep spinning, so I can just exist in it without the pressure of having to do more.

But deep down, I know that's not enough. I want more. I've always wanted more. It's just... hard to get there when your own mind is working against you.

There was a time when I thought I wouldn't make it. I'll never forget those nights where it felt like the only way to escape the pain was to make it stop—permanently. I came close, too close. But something held me back, something deep inside that refused to give up, even when everything else in me wanted to.

That something, that stubborn spark of hope, is why I'm still here. And now, I realize that surviving those moments didn't make me weak. It made me stronger than I ever thought I could be. But the battle doesn't end just because I made it through one dark night. It's a lifelong fight. Some days are harder than others, but I'm still here. And I think that's worth something.

I wish I could say I've figured it all out by now, but that's not true. My mental health is a constant work in progress. I've learned that there isn't some grand finish line where I'm suddenly "healed" or "fixed." I have good days and bad days. And I've learned to take it one step at a time.

Therapy helps when I can bring myself to go. It's not magic, but it gives me tools, ways to cope. It helps me unravel the tangled mess of thoughts in my head and make sense of things, little by little. And medication... well, it's complicated. I hated the idea at first, like it admitted defeat. But I've come to realize that it's not about giving up. It's about giving myself the best chance at living the life I deserve.

And I do deserve it. That's a hard thing to admit sometimes, but I'm learning to believe it. I deserve to be happy. I deserve to feel okay. I deserve to love myself, even on the days when I can't stand the person I see in the mirror.

It's not easy, though. The stigma around mental health is still so heavy. People don't talk about it enough, and when they do, it's always in whispers or with judgmental looks. I used to be afraid to admit that I struggled, afraid that people would think I was weak or that I wasn't trying hard enough. But now, I see how important it is to speak up.

Talking about it doesn't make me weak, it makes me human. And I'm not alone. None of us are. There are so many people out there going through the same thing, feeling the same darkness, fighting the same fight. And if talking about it can help even one person feel a little less alone, then it's worth it.

So, here I am. Still fighting. Still learning. Still trying to figure out how to live with this shadow that follows me around. I've come to accept that it may never fully leave, but that doesn't mean it has to control my life.

As I sit here, staring out at the world beyond my window, I realize that today is just one moment in a much bigger journey. And that's okay. I don't have to have all the answers right now. I don't have to fix everything at once. I must keep going, keep taking those small steps forward, no matter how hard it gets.

Because at the end of the day, there's still hope. There's always hope.

I know it's hard to stop the negative words from creeping in. They've been with me for so long, they almost feel natural. But every morning, I'm learning to fight back. Instead of letting those thoughts take over, I remind myself of something small, something kind.

When the voice in my head tells me I'm not enough, I don't argue. I breathe. I sit with it, and then I whisper, *I'm trying*. Some days, that's all I can manage. And it's enough.

I've learned that words are magic, shaping the world around us. So, I'm choosing different words now. Words that lift me instead of pulling me down. I tell myself I'm worthy, that I deserve love and care, even when it feels hard to believe. Slowly, those words are becoming louder than the doubt.

On good days, I feel the shift. I stand a little taller, take on the world a little braver. But not every day is good. Some days, the weight of it all feels like too much. And on those days, it's okay to lie back down, pull the covers close, and just breathe.

It's okay to get back in bed.

Because healing isn't always about moving forward. Sometimes, it's about pausing, letting yourself be still, and knowing that's enough too.

It's funny how the mind can turn on you. One minute, you're okay functioning, smiling, pretending everything is fine. And the next, you're spiraling, drowning in a sea of emotions you can't control or understand. Today was one of those days. The anxiety crept up slow, like a predator stalking its prey, waiting for the perfect moment to strike. And when it did, it hit me hard.

The walls of my room felt like they were closing in on me. My breaths were shallow, quick, and uneven. My hands shook as I gripped the edges of the kitchen counter, trying to ground myself in the present moment. Not today.

I closed my eyes, trying to focus on my breathing like the therapist had taught me. *In through the nose. Hold. Out through the mouth.* I counted each breath, with my thoughts racing, a tangled mess of fears and doubts that wouldn't quiet down.

What if I never feel better? What if this is my life forever?

The thought alone, enough to send a fresh wave of panic crashing over me, and I clutched the counter tighter, my knuckles turning white.

The truth is this wasn't new to me. I've been here before. Too many times to count. Anxiety had been my companion for as long as I could remember, whispering lies in my ear, telling me I wasn't good enough, that I was broken, that I'd never be happy.

There were good days. Days when I could laugh and mean it, when the future didn't seem so bleak. But on days like today, it felt like the bad outweighed the good.

I knew I needed to pull myself out of it. I couldn't stay in this place, trapped in my own head, letting the fear and doubt consume me. Knowing and doing it were two very different things. It's hard to fight a battle when the enemy is inside your own mind.

Anxiety is this shadow that never fully leaves. It lingers, even in moments of quiet. It tells me to worry, to overthink, to doubt everything I'm doing. And then there's the depression, an anchor pulling me deeper whenever I try to stay afloat. Together, they're like echoes in my mind—loud, constant, and inescapable.

No matter how hard I fight, they always come back. They're there in silence, in the noise, in the spaces between every breath I take. Sometimes I wonder how long I can keep fighting, but I remind myself that I've made it this far. That's something, right? Honestly, how do you explain sadness that doesn't have a reason? How do you explain anxiety when nothing is technically wrong?

Over the years, I've had plenty of people tell me to "just be positive," as if that was the magic solution to everything. They don't get it. Staying positive isn't a choice I can make. It's a fight.

I take a deep breath, trying to shake off the fog.

Deep down, I know it's... hard to get there when your own mind is working against you.

That stubborn spark of hope is why I'm still here. And now, I realize that surviving those moments didn't make me weak. It made me stronger than I ever thought I could be. The battle didn't end because I made it through one dark night. It's a lifelong fight.

My mental health is a constant work in progress. I've learned, there isn't some grand finish line where I'm "healed" or "fixed." I have good days and bad days. And I've learned to take it one step at a time.

Therapy helps when I can bring myself to go. It's not magic, but it gives me tools, ways to cope. It helps me unravel the tangled mess of thoughts in my head and make sense of things, little by little. And medication... well, it's complicated. I hated the idea at first, like admitting defeat. I've come to realize it's not about giving up. It's about giving myself the best chance at living the life I deserve.

And I do deserve it. That's a hard thing to admit sometimes, but I'm learning to believe it. I deserve to be happy, to feel okay, to love myself, even on the days when I can't stand the person I see in the mirror.

The stigma around mental health is still so heavy. People don't talk about it enough, and when they do, it's always in whispers or with judgmental looks. I used to be afraid to admit that I struggled, afraid people would think I was weak, or I wasn't trying hard enough. Now, I see how important it is to speak up.

Talking about it doesn't make me weak, it makes me human. And I'm not alone. None of us are. There are so many people out there going through the same thing, feeling the same darkness, fighting the same fight. And if talking about it can help even one person feel a little less alone, then it's worth it.

So, here I am. Still fighting, learning, and trying to figure out how to live with this shadow following me around. I've come to accept it may never fully leave, but it doesn't mean it will control my life.

I don't have to have all the answers right now. I don't have to fix everything at once. I must keep going, keep taking those small steps forward, no matter how hard it gets.

Because at the end of the day, there's still hope. There's always hope.

I know it's hard to stop the negative words from creeping in. They've been with me for so long, they almost feel natural. But every morning, I'm learning to fight back. Instead of letting those thoughts take over, I remind myself of something small, something kind.

When the voice in my head tells me I'm not enough, I don't argue. I breathe. I sit with it, and then I whisper, *I'm trying.* Some days, that's all I can manage. And it's enough.

I've learned that words are magic, shaping the world around us. So, I'm choosing different words now. Words that lift me instead of pulling me down. I tell myself I'm worthy, that I deserve love and care, even when it feels hard to believe. Those words are becoming louder than the doubt.

On good days, I feel the shift. I stand a little taller, take on the world a little braver. On the bad days, it's okay to lie back down, pull the covers close, and get back in bed. Sometimes, it's about pausing, letting yourself still, and knowing that's enough too but not today. I had to move.

"Jess?" Esther's voice broke through the fog, grounding me for just a moment. She stood in the doorway, arms crossed, her brow furrowed as she studied me.

I forced myself to straighten, loosening my death grip on the counter. "Hey."

Her eyes narrowed, unconvinced. "What's going on?"

"Nothing," I muttered, glancing down at the countertop.

"Nothing," she repeated, stepping into the room. "You're shaking like a leaf, and your voice is all over the place. That doesn't scream 'nothing.'"

I stiffened, refusing to meet her gaze.

"You're spiraling again," she said, setting the mug down and crossing the room. Her hand touched my arm, firm and steady. "Talk to me, Jess."

I shook my head, my voice stuck somewhere between my lungs and my throat. Her gaze didn't waver, though, and she pulled out one of the barstools, sitting down beside me.

"You have to stop letting this eat you alive," she said gently. "It's not going to win unless you let it."

I exhaled shakily, finally finding my words. "It feels like it's already won," I admitted, my fingers flexing against the counter. "I can't shake it today. Everything feels... too much."

Her lips pressed into a thin line, and she leaned back, studying me. "You know what helps you," she said after a moment. "But you're letting it pin you here."

I didn't respond. She wasn't wrong, but it didn't make the mountain of anxiety seem any smaller. Esther let the silence hang for a moment before her tone shifted, a little lighter.

"Hey, what about Kathy's thing tonight? Are you still planning to go?"

The question felt like a punch to the gut. I had almost forgotten about Kathy's film festival—almost. It had lingered in the back of my mind all morning, tangled up with my guilt. I nodded stiffly, more out of obligation than certainty.

"Jess," Esther said, her voice firmer now. "Do you really think pushing yourself like this is a good idea? If you're feeling this way, maybe it's better to sit this one out. Kathy will understand."

"No," I said, the word sharp and immediate, surprising even myself. I turned to face her fully, finally pulling my hands away from the counter. "I have to go. I can't let this stop me. Not again."

Her brows shot up, but she didn't argue right away. Instead, she studied me with that infuriating, knowing look she always wore when she was about to challenge me. "What are you trying to prove?"

"I'm not trying to prove anything," I said, my voice faltering slightly. "I just... I don't want this to control me anymore."

Esther sighed, shaking her head. "That's easier said than done, Jess. I'm not saying you shouldn't push through sometimes, but what happens if you get there and it's too much?"

"Then I'll deal with it," I said firmly. "I'll figure it out."

Esther watched me for a long moment before sighing again. "Okay," she said.

I said, meeting her gaze. "I'll be okay."

Her lips twitched into a faint smile, though her eyes stayed cautious. "You're stubborn, you know that?"

"I've been told."

"Jess, maybe you shouldn't go. If you're feeling like this—"

"I'm going," I cut in, the words tumbling out before I could think. My voice wavered, but I held onto the conviction in my chest.

Esther frowned, leaning against the counter across from me. "Why push yourself? Kathy will understand. She'd rather have you take care of yourself than show up and spiral."

My fists clenched at my sides, frustration boiling to the surface. "Because it's not about whether she'll understand. I promised her

I'd be there. She's been looking forward to this for weeks. I'm not going to let her down because of... this."

"'This' being your anxiety?" she asked, her voice softer now. "Jess, it's not letting her down if you need to take a step back. You're allowed to have boundaries."

I shook my head. "It's not about boundaries. It's about not letting it win. If I let it stop me now, what's next? Skipping Christine's texts because I'm too in my head? Canceling therapy because I can't deal with people that day?" I sighed, running a hand through my hair. "If I let it control me, it's just going to keep taking."

Esther's lips pressed into a thin line as she watched me. Her silence felt like both judgment and understanding, and it only made my chest tighten more. Finally, she spoke. "You're sure about this?"

"I have to be," I said. "If I give up every time it gets hard, I'll never get out of this cycle."

She exhaled, long and slow, and nodded. "Okay. But if you go and it gets to be too much, promise me you'll step outside or text me. Don't just push through and burn out."

"I promise," I said, the word feeling heavier than it should.

Esther picked up the mug she'd set on the counter and held it out to me. "Drink this before you do anything else. You need to breathe."

I took the mug, the warmth seeping into my palms as I stared at her. "Thank you."

"For what?"

"For being here. For not letting me talk myself into a hole."

She shrugged. "That's what friends do. Now, go show that anxiety, isn't the boss of you." She laughed under her breath and picked up her mug again, giving my shoulder a reassuring squeeze before heading back to the living room. I stayed rooted to the spot for a moment, letting the quiet settle over me again. Her words lingered in my mind, both comforting and challenging.

As the day stretched on, I found myself pacing the apartment, unable to focus on anything for more than a few minutes. The thought of the festival loomed large, both a source of excitement and dread. Kathy's short film was a deeply personal project raw, unflinching exploration of mental health and survival. I knew how much it meant to her, how much of herself she had poured into it. Missing it wasn't an option.

The hours leading up to the festival stretched long and heavy. Every task—choosing an outfit, fixing my hair—monumental, but I pushed through. Late afternoon, I managed to get ready as I stood in front of the mirror, adjusting my jacket for the third time, Esther appeared in the doorway again.

"You look good," she said, her voice free of the usual teasing edge. "Confident."

I laughed, though it came out more like a scoff. "I don't feel it."

"Fake it till you make it," she said, a small smile playing on her lips. "And remember think about Christine if you can't breathe. She makes you happy, right?"

Her mention of Christine brought a flicker of warmth to the surface, a reminder of the light I let back into my life. I nodded, a genuine smile tugging at my lips. "She does."

"Good," Esther said, stepping aside to let me pass. "Hold onto that."

By the time I stepped out of the apartment, the sun hung low in the sky, casting golden light across the city and painting the sky in shades of orange and pink. My chest still tight, but each step toward the subway was deliberate, an act of defiance against the anxiety that threatened to hold me back.

The train ride was a blur of movement and sound. By the time I reached the venue in Jersey City, my heart was pounding. The air buzzed with energy, voices blending as people milled about outside the theater. My palms were damp, and I wiped them on my black slacks, taking a deep breath before stepping inside.

The crowd, overwhelming, a sea of faces and conversations that made the air feel too thick to breathe. My chest tightened again, and for a moment, I considered turning back.

Then I saw her. Kathy stood near the entrance; her smile radiant as she greeted someone. She wore a simple red blouse and black leather pants, her natural waves flowing to her shoulders, her director pass hanging from her neck. When her eyes met mine, her face lit up.

"Jess!" She hurried over, pulling me into a hug. "You made it!"

"I wouldn't miss it," I said, my voice steady despite the nerves clawing at me.

Her excitement was infectious. She launched into a flurry of updates, her energy infectious as she spoke about the other films being shown, the directors she'd met, the nerves she was fighting. I nodded along, letting her words wash over me, focusing on her joy instead of the noise around us. Enough to push the anxiety to the edges of my mind.

As the screening began, we found seats near the back. The lights dimmed, and the theater fell silent. Kathy's film, *Morana*, was one of the first to play. The story unfolded on the screen, raw and powerful—a woman grappling with the aftermath of domestic violence, deciding whether to keep fighting or let go. The dialogue was sparse, the visuals stark, but every frame carried weight. It was beautiful, haunting, and unmistakably Kathy. I watched her film, marveling at the way she'd captured so much emotion with just her iPhone and a script she'd poured her soul into.

When the credits rolled, the audience erupted into applause. I turned to Kathy, tears in my eyes. "It was incredible," I whispered.

She smiled, but there was a flicker of nervousness in her expression. "You think so?"

"I know so."

The rest of the night passed in a haze of conversations. Kathy didn't win, but it didn't matter. Her film made an impact on me, and I couldn't have been prouder.

Later, as the crowd thinned, Kathy and I found a quiet corner outside the venue. The cool night air was a relief after the stuffy theater, and I leaned against the wall, letting the tension in my shoulders ease.

"You, okay?" Kathy asked, her voice soft.

I nodded. "Yeah. I am. Thanks for being... you."

She laughed, nudging me. "What does that even mean?"

"It means you remind me why it's worth pushing through the hard days," I said. "Watching your film, seeing you own your story—it makes me want to do the same."

Her smile softened. "You should. You have so much to say, Jess. So many people need to hear your story."

We talked late into the night, brainstorming ideas for how I could share my own journey. A short film? A memoir? By the time we said goodbye, my heart felt lighter, my steps surer. I wasn't just surviving anymore. I was moving forward.

9

Shadows Cast Light

M usic isn't just a hobby for me—it's in my bones, a part of who I am. I didn't just stumble upon it one day—it was already there, surrounding me, shaping me, thanks to my family. My father and grandfather were both accomplished musicians, well-respected for their talents. Growing up, our home was filled with the sounds of guitar strings, soulful singing, and the laughter of late-night jam sessions.

My earliest memories are filled with the sight of my father sitting on the edge of his chair, his fingers dancing across the strings of his guitar. My grandfather would often join him, their music creating an effortless harmony that seemed to make the world outside fade away. There were no formal lessons for me. I learned by watching, listening, and absorbing the rhythm that filled our home like air. The way they connected through their instruments, through the melodies they shared, it was like witnessing magic.

At family gatherings, they were always the center of attention, performing together, making everyone laugh, cry, or dance. It wasn't about being on stage or receiving applause, it was about connection. And as a little girl, I wanted so badly to be a part of that. I would sneak into their practice sessions, pretending to play along with a makeshift microphone or a toy guitar, lost in the music. It made me feel alive.

As I got older, I became more involved, learning bits and pieces from both my father and grandfather. They never pushed me, never forced me to take lessons or practice for hours like some other kids I knew. Instead, they let me explore music in my own way. Some days, I'd sit quietly by their side, just watching their fingers move, trying to memorize every chord, every note. Other days, I'd grab my father's old guitar and experiment, letting my fingers stumble across the strings until I found something that sounded halfway decent.

My father, though, was a perfectionist. While he never pressured me to pursue music professionally, I could see the way his eyes lit up when I got something right, and the way his brow furrowed when I didn't quite hit the mark. He had high standards, not just for himself but for anyone who tried to step into the world of music with him. But despite that, he was patient. He would sit with me for hours, helping me refine the smallest details until I could play a chord cleanly or match the rhythm of one of his songs.

My grandfather, on the other hand, was more laid-back, more focused on the joy of it all. He'd tell me stories about the old days, about playing in crowded bars and open-air festivals back in Puerto Rico, where music was as much a part of the culture as the air they breathed. He had an old record player, and sometimes, we'd sit together in the basement, listening to his old records, letting the music wash over us like a wave. "Listen with your heart, mija," he'd say, placing his hand over his chest. "That's where the real music comes from."

When I was about 12, my grandfather fell ill. He couldn't play as much, and eventually, he couldn't play at all. Watching him lose the ability to do what he loved most was heartbreaking, especially for my father. I could see it in the way his smile faltered, in the way his own playing became less frequent, less joyful. Music had been their bond, and with my grandfather's illness, that connection seemed to fray.

When my grandfather passed away, it felt like the music in our home went with him. My father's guitar stayed in its case often, and I found myself avoiding the basement where we used to sit and listen to records. It was too quiet. Too empty.

But even though the music had faded, it never truly disappeared.

Years later, I found myself returning to music in a way I hadn't expected. In 2023, I started working with an online radio station, helping with promotions and events. At first, it felt like just another job, something to pass the time. But as I got deeper into work, I realized that the passion I had for music as a child had never really gone away—it had just been lying dormant, waiting for the right moment to resurface.

Working with the station reconnected me to that part of my life. I wasn't performing like my father or grandfather had, but I was still part of the music world, helping bring people together through the power of sound.

There were nights when I'd sit at my desk, headphones on, listening to new tracks sent in by local musicians. It reminded me of sitting in the basement with my grandfather, letting the music carry me away. And every now and then, when I closed my eyes, I could almost hear his voice, telling me to listen with my heart.

Being part of the station has reignited something in me. It's not about becoming a performer or chasing the spotlight, like it was for my father or grandfather. It's about finding my own way to stay connected to the music that shaped me, that continues to shape me. Even though I've chosen a different path than they did, I still carry their legacy with me.

Music, in its own way, has always been there to guide me through the darkest times. It helped me cope with the loss of my grandfather, and it helped me find my way back when I thought I had lost that part of myself forever. Now, as I sit in front of my computer, working on the next event or listening to the next new artist, I know that the music hasn't left me. It never will.

The shadows of the past may still linger, but with music, I've found my way to cast a little light.

As I immersed myself in the world of online radio, I realized that my connection to music could transcend by promoting artists or curating playlists. It could serve as a platform for sharing stories and connecting with others who might be searching for their own light in the shadows. That's when the idea for my podcast, *Uncut and Unfiltered*, began to take shape.

As I dove deeper into podcasting, I realized it wasn't just about sharing music or talking to artists, it was about speaking my truth and creating a space where others could do the same. That's when *Uncut and Unfiltered with Jerzey Jess* was born. The concept was straightforward: no filters, no holding back, just raw, honest conversations about the things that matter—sexual abuse, addiction, mental health, relationships, and everything in between.

I wanted to create a space where real stories could be told, where those of us who've been through hell and back could sit down and talk openly about our struggles and the steps we've taken toward healing. It's never easy to bare your soul, but I've learned that when you do, you give others permission to do the same.

The topics I tackle aren't easy ones. They're heavy, raw, and, often, uncomfortable. But that's why *Uncut and Unfiltered* exist: to talk about what others might not want to or feel like they can't. We live in a world where it's still tough to openly discuss things like sexual abuse and mental health, and I wanted to break that silence. Silence was what held me back for so long—it kept me imprisoned in my own pain, my own confusion. And I figured if I could break through that silence, maybe others could too.

That's how it started—just me, speaking into a microphone, recording late at night when the world was quiet, and my thoughts were the loudest. My first episode wasn't perfect, but it was honest. It was me laying it all out there—my struggles with addiction, how I drowned myself in drugs and alcohol to escape the memories of abuse, the battles with depression that sometimes made getting out of bed feel like an insurmountable task. There was nothing polished or rehearsed about it. I let the words spill out because I had spent years bottling them up.

I remember the first episode—just me and a microphone, nerves frayed, unsure how it would be received. But as I spoke, sharing the darkest parts of my past, it felt like weight lifting. And the messages started coming in, people who resonated with my words, who found comfort in knowing they weren't alone. That's when I knew I had something real.

Every episode has been a continuation of that first step, a space to talk about the things most people shy away from. It's become a journey, not just for me, but for everyone who tunes in. Whether it's discussing the challenges of mental health or sharing experiences of love and loss, *Uncut and Unfiltered* has become more than just a podcast—it's a lifeline, a community of people who are choosing to face their pain and find healing in the process.

While I sometimes think about expanding the podcast, maybe adding interviews with artists or delving into new topics, for now, my focus is on speaking my truth and helping others speak theirs.

It's not just about me anymore, it's about the conversations we all need to have, the truths we all need to share, and the healing we all deserve.

And something remarkable happened: people listened. Not only did they listen, but they reached out. They told me that my story sounded like theirs, that they had experienced similar things but had never spoken about it. I realized I wasn't just talking to the void. I was talking to people who were grappling with the same demons, the same dark memories, and who needed to hear that they weren't alone.

That's what *Uncut and Unfiltered* became—a space where people could find solidarity in their suffering, a place where we could talk about what really goes on behind closed doors. I'm not here to sugarcoat anything. When I talk about sexual abuse, I talk about the pain, the confusion, and the long journey to reclaiming my body and mind. When I talk about addiction, I delve into how it consumed years of my life, how it pulled me down to my lowest point, and how every day of recovery is still a battle.

But it's not all darkness. One of the most important things about *Uncut and Unfiltered* is that while we address the hard stuff, we also talk about hope. We talk about survival and resilience. We talked about healing and growth. The show isn't just a place for people to dwell on the past; it's about acknowledging that while the past shapes us, it doesn't define us. It's about moving forward.

As the episodes grew, so did the conversations. I began inviting guests onto the show—people who had their own stories to tell. Some had been through abuse, others had battled addiction, and some were navigating the complex waters of mental health. And every story had its own unique thread, but at the core, there was always that shared experience of fighting through the pain and coming out the other side, however battered and bruised. We laughed together, cried together, and more importantly, we shared truths that needed to be spoken.

I remember one episode of the podcast that will always stay with me. It started like any other recording—sitting across from a guest, mic set up, the air thick with anticipation of the conversation that would unfold. But something about this episode felt different. As my guest started speaking, I could sense a weight in her words, a heaviness that hadn't been there when we had casually chatted before the recording. It wasn't long before the real reason for that weight started to emerge.

She began with the story of her childhood; one marked by expectations and a sense of responsibility that no child should carry. As the eldest sibling, she learned early on how to be the protector. She described those years like they were a kind of training ground, one where she had to be strong and vigilant, ensuring that what had happened to her wouldn't happen to anyone else in her family. Abuse had shaped her world, but she had sworn it would never touch her siblings. That role as protector became her identity, and she clung to it tightly, thinking that strength was the only way she could survive.

As she spoke, her words wrapped around me, pulling me into her story. The way she described wearing a mask of strength hit so close to home. I, too, had learned how to wear that mask, how to pretend that everything was fine when I was falling apart inside. Listening to her talk about carrying the weight of her family's emotions, I could feel the parallels between our lives, though she didn't know that yet.

She continued, her voice quieter now, almost as if the memories themselves had become too loud in her mind. "I thought if I stayed strong, if I never let anyone see the cracks, I could control it. I could keep it all inside and never let it affect anyone else." She paused, her hands fidgeting with the edge of her sleeve. "But it was eating me alive. I couldn't hold it all together."

I felt my throat tighten as she went on. She spoke about how, as the years went by, that mask started to crumble. Being the strong one was exhausting, and no one around her saw the strain it put on her. Because she was always the protector, no one thought of asking if she needed help. They assumed she had everything under control, even when her world was spiraling.

She went on, her voice cracking slightly. "I didn't want to be seen as a victim," she said, her hands gripping the arm of the chair. "I thought if I stayed strong, if I didn't let anyone see the cracks, I could control it. I could keep it all inside and make sure it never touched anyone else. My siblings didn't need to know, and my friends didn't either. If I told anyone, I'd lose that control."

That hit me hard. It was the same reason I had stayed silent for so long about my own abuse—because I didn't want to be seen as damaged, broken, or weak. The parallels between our stories were unsettling yet comforting. Here was guest, someone I had admired for her strength, revealing that her strength was the very thing that had held her hostage.

She described how that need to stay strong had started to wear her down. Over the years, she kept everything inside, refusing to ask for help, refusing to let anyone in. She became so accustomed to being the rock for everyone else that when she began to crumble, no one noticed. No one knew the battles she was fighting because she never let them.

And then she crashed.

She hit rock bottom when the weight of it finally became too much. "I didn't want to live anymore," she said, her voice barely a whisper. "I thought that if I disappeared, no one would miss me, and at least I wouldn't have to keep pretending." I saw the tears welling in her eyes, and I felt my own heart ache, knowing exactly what it was like to feel that kind of despair.

She spoke about her breaking point—the moment when everything she had been holding in finally became too much. She couldn't be the protector anymore. She couldn't be the strong one. The weight of her past trauma collided with the present, and she found herself in a deep depression. She stopped wanting to live, convinced that she had failed at everything she had spent years holding together.

As I listened, my heart felt like it was in a vice. It was painfully familiar—the way you think you're holding everything up, only to realize that it's all been slowly crumbling around you. She would lie in bed for days, feeling like a failure, not just to herself but to everyone around her. The woman who had always been so full of life, who made everyone feel like they belonged, had fallen apart.

But then, she spoke about finding the courage to reach out for help. "I realized I couldn't do it alone anymore," she said. "I had spent so long protecting everyone else that I forgot it was okay to ask for help, that it was okay to not be the strong one all the time." The #MeToo movement had given her a sense of belonging, seeing so many women come forward with their stories, their truths, it sparked something inside of her. It was a reminder that she wasn't alone and that she didn't have to be silent anymore.

As she shared this part of her journey, I felt the weight of her words settling deep into my own bones. The stories were different, but the pain, the silence, and the need for strength were all too familiar.

And then, as we were nearing the end of the recording, she said something that made my heart stop.

"You know," she said, "you never really know what someone is going through. People always thought I had it all together, but they had no idea what I was hiding."

I sat there, stunned. It hit me all at once. The voice, the story, the strength, this wasn't just another guest. This was Kathy. My Kathy. The girl from middle school who I had always looked up to, who I thought was untouchable. She had been the beacon of strength and confidence back then, the girl who made me feel like I wasn't so alone when I was just starting to navigate my own struggles. And all this time, she had been carrying her own pain, her own burdens, just like me.

I looked across the table at her, the reality of it settling in. I had always admired her, always thought she was the strong one, the one who had it all figured out. And yet, here we were, years later, sharing our stories, finding out that we had been walking parallel paths of pain and healing all along.

The recording ended, but the silence between us was charged with everything we hadn't said yet. Kathy had been my friend, my role model, and now she was someone who understood the darkness in ways I never could have imagined. Our lives had been intertwined in more ways than either of us had known, and in that moment, I realized just how much we had both grown.

Kathy smiled at me, the weight of her story now lighter, shared between us. "I never wanted to be seen as a victim," she said quietly. "That's why I never told anyone. I didn't want pity or for people to see me as weak."

I nodded, understanding in a way that words couldn't quite capture. "I get it," I said. "I didn't want that either."

That day, sitting across from Kathy, I learned a powerful lesson. You never truly know what someone is going through. The people you think have it all together, the ones you admire and look up to, maybe fighting battles you can't even imagine. And sometimes, their stories mirror your own in ways that are both painful and beautiful.

Kathy and I shared something that day—a deep understanding of the strength it takes to face your past, to strip away the mask, and to show the world who you really are. It wasn't about being a victim. It was about reclaiming our stories and owning the truth of who we are, scars and all.

That episode wasn't just a podcast recording. It was a reminder that, even in our darkest moments, we are never truly alone. There is strength in vulnerability, and sometimes, the people we think are the strongest are the ones who need support the most. Sitting with Kathy taught me something important: you never truly know someone's story until they tell it. I had spent years looking up to Kathy, not realizing that she had been fighting her own battles all along. And that, I think, is the most important thing I've learned from doing this podcast. We all wear masks. We all hide parts of ourselves. But when we finally let those masks fall, we find connection, healing, and sometimes even deeper friendship.

As the podcast grew, I also began to touch on relationships—not just romantic ones, but friendships, family connections, and, most importantly, the relationship we have with ourselves. I talked about how, for years, I didn't value myself, how I allowed toxic relationships to define my worth. I spoke about the long journey toward self-acceptance, how learning to love myself was one of the hardest battles I'd ever fought. And through those conversations, I realized that a lot of people were struggling with the same thing. We all wear masks in some way, trying to be what we think others want us to be, but at what cost?

Through the podcast, I've found that the most important relationship we can have is the one we build with ourselves. When we start to peel back the layers of trauma, addiction, and pain, we're left with the raw, unfiltered version of who we are. And it's in that vulnerability that real healing begins.

One of the most beautiful things about *Uncut and Unfiltered* is the community that's grown around it. I never imagined that starting a podcast in my living room would lead to building such deep connections with people I've never even met in person. But every message I receive, every comment on an episode, reminds me that we're not alone in our struggles. There's strength in sharing our stories, and there's even more strength in listening to others.

And while the podcast has been an incredible journey of self-discovery and connection, I know this is just the beginning. My dream is to continue growing *Uncut and Unfiltered*, to keep having those tough, raw conversations, and to reach more people who need to hear that they're not alone. One day, I hope to expand it, maybe even invite some of the guests I've always wanted to have on, but for now, I'm content with the space we've created—a space of honesty, healing, and hope.

When I sign off at the end of each episode, I always remind my listeners of one thing: "You are not your pain. You are not your trauma. You are the strength that rises from it." And that's the message I want to leave with every single person who tunes in. Life is hard. Sometimes, it feels unbearable. But if there's one thing I've learned through my journey, it's that we have the strength to rise. We can come out of the darkness. We can heal. We can grow.

10

The Strength to Rise

The soft glow of the recording light flickered on, and I leaned into the microphone, feeling the familiar rush of excitement mixed with vulnerability. *"Welcome back to my podcast, everyone. I'm so grateful to have you here with me. Today's episode is a bit different—a moment of reflection on this journey we've shared together."*

I took a deep breath, letting the silence settle around me for a moment before I continued. *"When I think about the path I've walked, I'm reminded of the moments that felt like they would break me. There were days when I felt trapped, suffocated by a past I couldn't escape. The shadows of regret loomed large, wrapping around me like heavy fog. But through every struggle, I discovered something invaluable: the strength to rise."*

As I spoke, my mind drifted back to those early days of grappling with my trauma. I could still feel the weight of despair, the suffocating grip of fear, and the deep sense of isolation that clung to me. *"For so long, I believed that my pain defined me. I carried it like a badge, but I didn't realize it was holding me back. I felt like I was trapped in a cycle of shame and fear, spinning in circles until I was dizzy. Yet, with each brave confrontation of that darkness, I found a little more light illuminating the path ahead."*

I paused, letting my thoughts settle, and allowed myself to reflect on the progress I had made. *"There was a pivotal moment when I finally understood that my scars are not just remnants of pain; they are symbols of my resilience. Each scar tells a story of survival, of battles fought and won, even when victory seemed impossible."*

I closed my eyes for a moment, conjuring the image of my favorite childhood tree—a gnarled oak with branches that twisted toward the sky, each knot and scar a testament to its strength. *"Just like a tree, I realized that the storms I weathered only made me stronger, more deeply rooted in my sense of self."*

The studio felt intimate, as if I were sharing my heart with friends who truly understood. *"I remember a time when I stood on the edge of despair, feeling utterly alone. The night was dark, the kind of darkness that creeps into your bones and chills your spirit. But deep within me, a small flicker of hope ignited. It whispered that I was meant for something greater than the shadows that loomed over me. That whisper became a guiding force, encouraging me to take steps toward healing and I know that you can too."*

Those steps were often tentative. I remember taking a walk in the park, the fresh air biting my cheeks, and I found myself writing down my feelings on scraps of paper. Each word felt like a small act of defiance against the weight of my past. With every sentence, I reclaimed a piece of myself, transforming pain into expression.

I recalled the moments that marked my journey, the nights spent pouring my heart into journals, the pages stained with tears and ink, where I spilled my secrets like confessions to a silent witness. I remembered the conversations with friends who offered support, their words wrapping around me like a warm blanket on a cold night, and the unexpected encounters with strangers who shared their own stories of struggle. *"These experiences shaped me, showing me the beauty of connection and community."*

Each person I met added another layer to my understanding of resilience. There was the elderly woman at the café who told me about her struggles with loss, her laughter ringing through her tears. Her story reminded me that strength isn't always loud; sometimes, it's quiet perseverance. In those exchanges, I found not only solace but also a sense of belonging.

It became clear that I wasn't alone in my fight; many were grappling with their battles, and together, we formed a network of resilience.

Each story I heard fueled my resolve to rise. *"I became passionate about helping others, eager to be a voice for those who felt silenced. It was in this passion that I found purpose. My journey transformed into a mission to uplift and empower others, reminding them that they, too, possess the strength to overcome. This mission became a lighthouse in my life. I started volunteering at local shelters, sharing my story with those who felt lost. I realized that in opening my heart, I could shine a light for others navigating their own darkness. Each smile I received in return filled my spirit, reinforcing the belief that vulnerability could foster healing."*

As I reflected on my evolution, I felt a swell of gratitude for the people who stood by me. *"My fiancé, who walked beside me through the darkest valleys, has been a beacon of love and encouragement. Together, we've navigated the storms, showing me that love can heal, and I am forever grateful. I remember the countless nights we spent talking under the stars, sharing our dreams and fears. Her unwavering support felt like a lifeline, reminding me that I was never truly alone. Each word she spoke was a gentle reminder that even in chaos, love could flourish. Those moments became our sanctuary, a space where we could both be vulnerable without judgment."*

I could feel the warmth of that love surrounding me as I shared these thoughts. *"Love, as I learned, is not merely a fleeting emotion but a powerful force that binds us together. But it's not just about individual support; it's about community,"* I continued, reflecting on the countless moments that have shaped my understanding of connection. *"I've had the privilege of connecting with so many remarkable individuals along the way, each with a unique story to tell. There was Sarah, whose journey through addiction led her to become a passionate advocate for mental health awareness, reminding me that our struggles can fuel our purpose. And then there was Mark, a fellow survivor who used his art to express the pain of his past and inspire others to find their voice. These individuals transformed their pain into purpose, creating ripples of change in the world around them. Their courage inspires me daily, serving as a reminder that when we come together, we can amplify our voices and create a lasting impact."*

I leaned back in my chair, taking a moment to reflect on my commitment to uplift others. *"Every conversation, every shared story, has reinforced my belief that we all have the power to make a difference. Each of us possesses unique gifts that can light up the world, even in the smallest ways. Whether through art, advocacy, or simple acts of kindness, our voices matter."*

The importance of uplifting others weighed heavily on my heart. *"In a world that often feels divided, it's essential to remember that our differences are what make us strong. Each person carries their own story, their own experiences, and when we come together, we create a beautiful mosaic of humanity. This unity is where true strength lies."*

As I spoke, I could feel the energy in the room shift, an electric current of hope and determination coursing through me. *"I want you to know that it's okay to have days when you feel overwhelmed. It's okay to feel lost and uncertain. But remember, within you lies an incred-*

ible reservoir of strength. You have the ability to rise, to confront your fears, and to create a future filled with possibility."

I took a moment to let my words resonate, allowing silence to fill the space. *"Life can be unpredictable, and sometimes it may feel like the weight of the world is on your shoulders. But trust me, you have the resilience to bear it. There were times when I doubted my ability to overcome, yet here I am, standing tall and unbroken. And if I can do it, so can you. In those moments of doubt, I hope you find your own refuge, whether in writing, art, or the support of loved ones. The important thing is to keep moving forward."*

The final thoughts of my journey began to coalesce in my mind, and I felt a sense of closure washing over me. *"As I close this chapter of my story, I carry with me the lessons learned, the love shared, and the promise to continue rising. I aim to be a voice for those who may still be struggling, showing them that healing is possible and that they are not alone."*

With a heart full of gratitude, I spoke into the microphone as if speaking to a dear friend. *"Thank you for joining me on this journey. Your support and willingness to listen mean the world to me. Together, let's keep pushing forward, standing strong, and lifting each other up. Our stories matter, and through them, we can create a brighter, more compassionate world."*

I paused for a moment, letting the weight of my words sink in, then added, *"This is Jerzey Jess, signing off for now. Remember, you have the strength to rise, and I can't wait to see where your journey takes you. Until next time."*

I took a deep breath, a sense of calm washing over me as I settled into the quiet of my thoughts. Closing my eyes, I allowed my mind to drift into the future, a future that shimmered with promise and healing. I could finally see it clearly, a landscape painted with the vibrant colors of hope. The dark days that had once cloaked my life in shadows now felt distant, almost like a faded memory.

A surge of freedom enveloped me like warm sunlight breaking through morning fog. My feet pressed against solid ground, each step forward unburdened by shadows of the past. Struggles that once loomed like insurmountable walls now served as stepping-stones beneath me. Every scar, every memory, had forged my strength, transforming pain into something I could carry lightly, with grace.

The future stretched before me, vivid and alive. I envisioned gatherings with friends, faces glowing with laughter and warmth. We leaned close over steaming mugs, sharing stories not from a place of pain but of triumph. Connection filled the air, weaving joy and understanding between us. Here, love filled every space, as natural as breathing. I could feel the wholeness of a life shaped by healing—a life once imagined but now real, a place where laughter flowed easily, and peace settled deep in my bones.

Faces of listeners and readers appeared in my mind, people I'd never met but whose presence felt close. They, too, had reached for the light in my story, finding hope where I had searched desperately for it. I pictured someone finishing my book, taking a deep breath, and letting the smallest spark of hope ignite. That spark—my spark—would reach them, reminding them they weren't alone. My voice no longer needed to echo over airwaves; the impact lingered, unfolding within the lives of others.

In my vision, we gathered in circles, sharing stories openly, creating spaces to heal. People rose to speak, each voice steady, each word carrying a lifetime of courage. Together, we transformed pain into strength and isolation into community. Here, in these quiet circles, I felt connection like a live current, lifting us all, bringing us closer to healing.

HIDDEN SCARS - 139

I had given everything to my story and released it, creating space to live fully, untethered by old wounds. The work felt complete, but the journey continued, stronger and more beautiful than I had ever imagined.

With each breath, I felt lighter, the air filling with possibilities I could finally claim as my own. This was the life I had fought for, the future I now held close. Moving forward, I stepped into a light that carried joy, purpose, and love, painting each day with strength. Ready to live a story that was undeniably mine, I embraced it all—whole and unafraid.

This story isn't just mine. It belongs to every one of us who's ever struggled, fought, or dared to hope for something better. We've walked through fire and learned hard lessons, and I believe that those experiences can light the way forward—not just for ourselves, but for everyone around us.

So, I'm inviting you to join me in something bigger. Take a moment to pause and consider your own story. Think about the twists and turns, the challenges that have shaped you into who you are. Those moments, no matter how painful, are powerful. They are the foundation of a resilient, compassionate community world where every voice counts and every story matters. You, with all that you've been through, have the strength and wisdom to make a difference. You've lived through moments that could have broken you, but here you are, on the other side, and that matters.

Imagine what we could create together if each of us took one small step to help someone else. That's how real change begins—with simple, genuine acts of kindness and understanding. You don't need a grand plan or a perfect idea. Start with what you have, with what you know. Look around your community, see the people in your life who might need a hand. Maybe they're fighting silent battles, hiding behind polite smiles, just hoping someone will notice. Be that someone. Offer them a listening ear, a kind word, or simply your presence. Sometimes, knowing that someone else cares can be the spark that lights their way out of the dark.

Let me tell you what I imagine for us all—a future where sharing our stories isn't an exception but a norm, where vulnerability is celebrated, not hidden. A world where people can stand up and say, "This is who I am, and this is where I've been," without fear of judgment or rejection. We have the power to build that world, but it requires courage from each of us. It means stepping out of our comfort zones, speaking our truths, and being open to hearing others' truths, too.

And here's the thing: it's not always easy to reach out. We might worry about overstepping, or about facing rejection. I've been there, too, feeling that pull of fear when it's time to be vulnerable. But every time I pushed past it, every time I shared just a little more of myself, I felt the weight lift, and I saw that it wasn't just helping me—it was helping others find the courage to speak up, too. That's what I want for you. Let this be the start of something, not the end. Let this be the moment you decide to use your story as a source of strength, a beacon for others to follow.

I envision communities that gather, even in small ways, to connect and heal together. Imagine small circles in your neighborhood, in coffee shops or community centers, where people come together just to share and listen. Maybe it's a few friends who start opening about their experiences, or a group who decides to volunteer together. These spaces don't have to be perfect, just open. Imagine the impact of feeling supported, of knowing you don't have to face your struggles alone. That's the ripple effect I believe in—the one where we all play a part, no matter how small it might seem.

And it's not just about talking, it's about acting, too. Support your local initiatives, lend a hand with community efforts, speak up when someone needs a voice beside them. Together, we can create networks of support that lift people up, even if just for a moment, and help them find their own path forward. Every act counts, and even the smallest actions can build a wave of change.

The beauty of it all is that you don't have to be anyone other than who you are. Your story, your life, as it is right now, has the power to inspire. You're a living testament to the ability to rise even after life has tried to pull you down. Don't underestimate that. Let it shine. Be honest with yourself, and let others see that honesty. We live in a world where so many people hide behind masks, pretending to be okay. But if we can show up as we are, with all our flaws and fears, we create permission for others to do the same.

From here, I hope you feel inspired to carry the torch, to keep the conversation going, and to take your own steps toward healing. Let's continue this work together, finding ways to lift each other up, to be there even when it's uncomfortable or hard. Let's bring our stories to light, not for validation but to create understanding and compassion. This, I believe, is how we heal—not just individually, but collectively.

I want you to imagine a world where no one has to feel alone in their struggles. A world where people know there are others who understand, who have walked similar paths and survived. That's the world I dream of, and I know it's possible. But it's going to take each of us. You have a role to play, just as I do. Think of the power that lies in that simple truth. We're stronger than we know, and together, we can build something truly beautiful, a world where hope and healing aren't just dreams, but everyday realities.

So, here's my invitation to you, be brave. Step into your story, embrace it fully, and use it as a tool to connect, to inspire, to make a difference. You've come this far, and there's so much more ahead. Take this journey with me—let's build that world, one story, one action at a time. We've walked through darkness, and now it's time to bring that light to others.

As I come to the end of this chapter, a profound realization settles within me. Sharing my story—bearing my scars, recounting moments of darkness, and revealing my truth—has emerged as one of the most vulnerable and empowering experiences of my life. Each confrontation with my past and every acknowledgment of my fears propelled me toward embracing my authentic self, dismantling the barriers I had painstakingly built over the years. Telling my story has felt like an act of peeling back layers, not solely for my own healing, but in the hope that others might find echoes of their own journeys within mine.

In these moments of revelation, I discovered an unexpected lightness. With each truth I spoke, I reclaimed a part of myself. This ongoing journey has deepened my understanding of gratitude—for the raw honesty it demanded, for the courage it required to face my own shadows, and for the privilege of inviting you into those spaces with me.

Reflecting on the path I've traveled brings an almost surreal sense of peace. What began as a daunting, uneasy process—transforming my pain into words and offering pieces of my essence to the world—has ultimately forged my greatest source of strength. The journey to authenticity was not just about reconciling my sexuality or past; it became an exploration of the buried aspects of myself, confronting shame and disappointment along the way. In this exploration, I unearthed the truth that authenticity is a hard-won gift, earned by showing up for ourselves time and again, until there is nothing left to conceal. I've come to realize that my story does not need perfection; it simply needs to be my own.

In sharing my experiences, I've been privileged to witness a universal truth: we are all navigating life, each fighting our own invisible battles. There is no prescribed way to heal; there is only your way, and it is enough. If I could impart one final thought, it would be this: you possess everything within you to shape a life that feels whole and true. No matter what you have faced, no matter the darkness that has sought to dim your spirit, remember that it has not extinguished your light. Rather, it has transformed and fortified it in ways that may still be unfolding as you move forward.

You are both the sculptor and the stone, diligently chipping away at the parts of yourself that no longer serve you, revealing the inherent beauty that has always existed beneath the surface. When life feels heavy, when the weight of the world feels overwhelming, remember this moment. Recall the strength that has carried you through storms, that same heart beating through your most trying times, now filled with the wisdom, grace, and courage that only emerges through lived experience. Lean into that wisdom; trust that you are more than enough, even on the days when doubt and fear try to persuade you otherwise.

We often overlook the profound impact of small actions. The gentle reminders, the quiet acts of kindness, and the seemingly insignificant moments of connection—each of these is a ripple that can change the world, even when we cannot see it. So, take that first step, however small it may seem, toward the life you envision. Speak your truth, support those around you, and remember that every choice contributes to the world we are collectively building.

In the end, the impact of a single voice, a single story shared openly, can reach farther than we might ever realize. It's like dropping a stone into a vast, still lake; the ripples travel outward, touching places and people we may never encounter. Each story, each hard truth bravely spoken, becomes a source of strength not only for ourselves but for those who come after us, searching for a sense of belonging and a reminder that they are not alone.

For me, sharing my story felt like opening a window that had been closed for far too long, allowing fresh air and light to flood in where shadows once lingered. In embracing vulnerability, I discovered power, and in authenticity, I unearthed a freedom that cannot be replicated. I have learned that even the deepest wounds can form the very foundation upon which we build the lives we are meant to lead, if only we allow them to.

If there's one truth I have come to know, it's that courage doesn't always roar. Sometimes it is the quiet resolve to keep moving forward, to show up for ourselves and for others, and to believe that the best parts of our story are still unfolding. To everyone reading this, to those who have accompanied me on this journey, thank you. Thank you for listening, for holding space, and for being willing to witness the raw, unrefined parts of a life reclaimed.

Let this be our shared promise: to continue speaking, to keep listening, and to lift each other along the way. Because in the end, we are all just voices, longing to be heard, seeking connection, and leaving ripples that remind the world we were here, that we mattered.

I may not know where your journey will take you, but I have faith that you will find the light you seek, even amidst the heaviness or uncertainty. Thank you for allowing me to be a part of your life, if only for a moment. Together, let's step into our truths and continue this journey, one story at a time.

About the Author

Jessica C. Perez's life is a testament to the power of perseverance, self-discovery, and the unbreakable will to rise above life's darkest moments. Born in Passaic, New Jersey, and raised in the vibrant community of Clifton, Jessica's journey has been one of profound transformation. Despite the love and warmth she received from her family, her early years were marked by deep personal challenges, trauma and struggles with addiction that threatened to overshadow her potential.

Through the depths of these struggles, Jessica found an inner strength that defied the odds. She emerged from the shadows of her past, fueled by the support of a few key people who never let her forget her worth. These relationships, along with her fierce determination, guided her toward a path of healing and redemption. Jessica's experience, though filled with pain, also ignited a passion in her, to not only survive but to thrive, and to use her voice for the betterment of others.

In her memoir, *Hidden Scars*, Jessica bares her soul, sharing a raw and intimate look at her life's journey. It's more than just a memoir; it's a call to those who feel lost or broken, a reminder that no matter how deep the pain runs' healing is always possible. Through her candid storytelling, Jessica offers readers a beacon of hope, showing that our scars can become the foundation of our strength.

Now residing in sunny Florida with her fiance Christine and their dog, Jessica continues to make an impact far beyond the pages of her book. As a passionate advocate for mental health awareness and LGBTQI+ rights, she uses her platform to uplift those facing similar struggles, reminding them that they are never alone. Her advocacy work is deeply personal, driven by a desire to create spaces where people feel seen, heard, and accepted for who they are.

Jessica also finds joy in sharing her message of hope through her podcast, where she explores topics such as mental health, self-empowerment, and personal growth. With each episode, she invites listeners to join her on a journey of healing, breaking down stigmas and offering insights from her own life. Her voice has become a source of comfort and empowerment, reminding people that while the journey toward self-acceptance may be long, it is always worth it.

In both her personal and professional life, Jessica embodies resilience, courage, and compassion. Whether through her writing, her advocacy, or her podcast, she is committed to helping others rise above their circumstances, embrace their truths, and find the strength to create their own narratives of healing and empowerment.

www.ingramcontent.com/pod-product-compliance
Lightning Source LLC
Chambersburg PA
CBHW061804120626
46550CB00005B/2126